How to Trace the History of Your Car

A Guide to Motor Vehicle Registration Records in Great Britain, Ireland, the Isle of Man and Channel Islands

Philip Riden

HOW TO TRACE THE HISTORY OF YOUR CAR

A Guide to Motor Vehicle Registration Records
in Great Britain, Ireland, the Isle of Man
and Channel Islands.

First published in Great Britain in February 1991 by Academy Books Limited
Copyright © Philip Riden 1991

ISBN 1 873361 05 X

Published and distributed by:
Academy Books Limited
35 Pretoria Avenue
London E17 7DR

Direct sales enquiries to:
Tel: 081 521 7647
Fax: 081 503 6655

Printed in Great Britain by:
Hillman Printers (Frome) Ltd
Frome
Somerset

1st reprint April 1991

Cover picture:

*This photograph is of the first car to carry the registration number DC1, which was
the first number issued in Middlesbrough in the early part of this century. The driver is
Mr Scobie Smith, a local businessman. The car has been lost although Mr Smith's son
retained the registration for many years and it was later transferred to a firm in
Blackpool. Middlesbrough is unique in having preserved pictorial as well as documentary evidence of early local vehicles.*

Foreword

by David Adcock

President and Immediate Past Chairman of the Daimler & Lanchester
Owners' Club

In **How to Trace the History of Your Car** Philip Riden has
analysed and chronicled the present system of motor vehicle registration and, for the first time, explained how the motorist goes about veri-
fying the history of his vehicle. A comprehensive survey of the
remaining records in the UK, the Isle of Man, the Channel Islands and
the Republic of Ireland includes a complete directory of addresses and
telephone numbers of where surviving archives can be found.

This book is invaluable for anyone owning or contemplating the
purchase of a vehicle where the documentary evidence is incomplete,
and to Club Secretaries, local historians, historical societies and
archivists.

I have no hesitation in commending this book to anyone with an
interest in older vehicles and local history. It is particularly useful to
owners of vehicles which were off the road when the present system
was established in the 1970s who have suffered most and benefitted
least from the current system of vehicle registration.

David Adcock

Contents

Introduction

This book is a guide to the main sources available to motoring enthusiasts, local historians and others interested in tracing the history of a motor vehicle used in Great Britain, Ireland, the Isle of Man or Channel Islands since registration began early this century. It is especially useful for owners of cars which were off the road when the present system was established in the 1970s who now wish to have an original number restored to such vehicles, since full details are given where local authority registration records can be found.

Vehicle registration, using index marks made up of letters and numbers, was introduced into the United Kingdom in 1903 and was for many years administered by the larger local authorities until the Vehicle and Driving Licences Act of 1969 paved the way for sweeping changes. The registration of vehicles and licensing of drivers was transferred from the local authorities, which since 1920 had acted as agents of the Minister of Transport, to the department itself, which established a single computerised record of both vehicles and drivers in Swansea. In place of nearly two hundred offices previously maintained by local councils, the department retained only some 80 public service points, on the assumption that most motorists, as well as the trade, would in future deal with the Driver and Vehicle Licensing Centre by post or through the Post Office.

Centralisation on this scale clearly had major implications for the survival and preservation of the records kept by over a hundred local authorities since 1903. Unfortunately, the transfer of responsibility, originally intended to be complete by 1 April 1971, extended for another seven years, during which time the local authorities acted as agents for the Department of the Environment. The transitional period thus coincided with that of 1972-4, during which local government as a whole was radically remodelled in England and Wales, and 1973-5, when similar changes took effect in Scotland. Large quantities of material, including in some cases the entire contents of a local taxation office, were lost during this period.

Since the late 1970s, interest in restoring and running older cars has grown, together with a corresponding interest in their history, for which local authority registration records are an important source.

These records have thus become the subject of considerable discussion in the classic car world, especially where owners of cars not included in the DVLC database have sought to have original registration marks restored to vehicles which have been off the road for some years. The value of the records for the history of car-ownership in particular areas or the history of some of the smaller vehicle manufacturers is now more widely appreciated.

This introduction sets out the administrative history of motor vehicle registration in both Great Britain and Ireland since 1903; describes what records were created by local authorities, and outlines what survives today. There then follows a complete list of all index marks used in Great Britain and Ireland, with details of what records are known to survive for each mark and where they may be found.

In compiling this book, I have been helped by many archivists who have responded to my enquiries about their holdings of registration records. The list includes staff of every local authority record office in England, Scotland and Wales, the Public Record Office at Kew, the Scottish Record Office in Edinburgh and the Public Record Office of Northern Ireland in Belfast. For the position in the Republic of Ireland, I am indebted to almost every county librarian or motor taxation officer, to several local archivists and to the Director of the National Archives in Dublin. Further help has come from the Manx Museum and the Vehicle Registration Officers of Jersey and Guernsey. Both the Driver and Vehicle Licensing Centre at Swansea and their counterparts in Belfast and Dublin have kindly answered queries about present-day arrangements.

This survey was carried out during the summer of 1990 and should accurately reflect the location of documents at that date. If any reader discovers other registration records not listed here, or finds that material has been moved to another office since this guide was compiled, or simply notices a mistake in the text, I should be most grateful for details so that any later edition can be corrected.

January 1991
Philip Riden

2

Vehicle Registration Records:
A Brief History

The Motor Car Act of 1903

The registration of motor vehicles, and the licensing of their drivers, was introduced throughout the United Kingdom by the Motor Car Act of 1903. Registration of 'light motors' (weighing less than three tons) was provided for in the Highways Act of 1896, but not implemented; conversely the Locomotives Act of 1898, which dealt with heavier road vehicles, did establish a system of registration and licensing (but not numbering), which was entrusted to local authorities. Despite these precedents, the registration provisions of the 1903 bill, like the rest of the measure, aroused considerable controversy, with complaints that to number private cars was to treat them as though they were hackney carriages or omnibuses. It says much for contemporary views of the likely growth of car ownership that opponents seriously suggested that private cars should carry names, like boats or houses, rather than numbers. An effective system of identification, capable of more or less infinite expansion, was however essential if the other provisions of the 1903 Act and earlier legislation relating to the speed at which vehicles might be driven were to be enforced by the police. It was to assist the police in this task, rather than as a means of raising revenue, that registration, using a system of index marks, was introduced in 1903, together with the licensing of drivers (but with no test as to their proficiency).

The Motor Car Act merely established the general principles of registration and licensing; detailed arrangements for England and Wales were set out in the Motor Car (Registration and Licensing) Order issued by the Local Government Board on 19 November 1903, accompanied by a circular to local authorities explaining the new measure. Similar instruments were issued by the Scottish and Irish offices for the remainder of the United Kingdom. Both registration and licensing were entrusted to county and county borough councils in England and Ireland (counties and large burghs in Scotland). The local authorities were to open registers in a form prescribed in a schedule to the order for motorcars and motorcycles, with the option of keeping either a single set of books for both or two parallel series. The issue of driving licences was to be registered separately. A fee of 20s. was payable for each motorcar registered and 5s. for each motor-cycle; owners were to be supplied with a copy of the entry relating to their vehicle. Changes of ownership, or the permanent export or scrapping of vehicles was to be noted and, in the latter two cases, a number thus becoming available mght be reallocated to another vehicle.

The registration numbers themselves were to be displayed on plates mounted vertically at the front and rear of motorcars (arrangements were modified somewhat for motorcycles), or might be painted on the vehicles themselves in the same form as a plate. The size and shape of the plate were set out in a schedule to the order, which established the pattern of white letters on a black ground that was to remain familiar for nearly seventy years. The plates were to be illuminated at night, either by reflection or transparency; in practice the first solution came to be universally adopted. Councils were permitted under the order to supply and charge for number plates but few, if any, appear to have done so. Finally, the order also established the 'general identification plate' system, whereby motor dealers might be assigned a number which they could attach temporarily to a vehicle which was being delivered to or collected from a customer. Such 'trade plates', as they have long been known, were to be listed in a separate register and dis-tinctively coloured: again, the familiar white lettering on a red ground still in use today dates from as long ago as 1903.

The numbering system itself set out in the order was kept as simple as possible and was probably envisaged at the time as adequate to meet any foreseeable increase in the number of vehicles on the road. Each registration authority was allocated an index mark consisting of one or two letters. Initially, 24 single-letter marks were introduced (I and Q being omitted to avoid confusion with J and O), together with two-letter combinations as far down the alphabet as those beginning with F. In addition, special arrangements were made to identify vehicles registered in Scotland, where all marks were to include the letters G, S or V, and Ireland, which was to use I (although only in combination with another letter) and Z. It is characteristic of the attitude of the Local Government Board of the day, as well as that of Walter Long, its President, that no similar concession was made to Wales, which was treated simply as part of England. Had registration been introduced only a few years later, after the election of the Liberal government in 1906, when for the first time the separate identity of Wales began to be recognised officially in numerous ways, it seems likely that index marks including the letter W would have been reserved for the seventeen Welsh registration authorities, which in the event were never accorded special recognition. Each registration authority was initially allocated a single mark and, in some rural counties and small county boroughs, this provision sufficed right down to the abolition of local authority registration. In other cases, new combinations of letters were issued at intervals by order.

The LGB regulations of 1903 enjoined local authorities to issue registration marks consisting of the index letter (or letters) followed by a number. This was to form a simple series from 1 onwards, although authorities which chose to register cars and motorcycles separately issued two parallel series, with the result that (until the system was changed under the 1920 Roads Act) the same registration mark might be borne by both a car and a motorcycle. The regulations asked local authorities not to issue numbers beyond 999 for any one index mark and offered to allocate a new two-letter mark when a council exhausted its initial block of numbers. In practice, although a number of additional index marks were allocated in the period up to 1920, local authorities issued numbers up to 9999 to provide greater scope for expanding the system.

In general, despite the opposition to vehicle numbering expressed when the 1903 bill was introduced, once it had passed into law the measure appears to have been implemented without difficulty. In any case, the Act made it an offence not to display a number plate in the prescribed manner or to use an unregistered vehicle on the highway except to drive to a registration authority's office. The only problem seems to have arisen with two-letter marks which were construed as offensive. Thus, when BF was allocated to Dorset, local automobilists objected and, in December 1904, the Local Government Board was persuaded to issue FX to the county instead, giving owners the option of retaining their BF number or exchanging it for a new one prefaced by FX. BF was not re-used in the 1921 numbering scheme. The only two-letter combination not issued by the LGB (or, after 1920, by the Ministry of Transport) to avoid giving offence appears to have been WC; curiously, no such inhibitions were felt about allocating VD to Lanarkshire. As a consequence of the decision to reserve certain letters for Scottish and Irish local authorities, the combinations GI, IG, VI, IV, SI and IS were not issued at all, nor was ZS, although many years later Co. Down was allocated SZ by the Northern Ireland Ministry of Transport.

The Act of 1903 came into effect on 1 January 1904 but, in the order issued the previous November, local authorities were instructed to open vehicle and driving licence registers at once (taking advantage of s. 37 of the Interpretation Act, 1889), since owners were free to apply for registration as soon as the bill became law. In most, if not all, counties, at least in England, there would already have been some vehicles on the road by the autumn of 1903 and so, in most books, the first few pages would have been taken up with the retrospective registration of vehicles which had already been in use for some time, rather than cars newly acquired in 1904.

The arrangements made under the 1903 Act continued to operate until just after the First World War, with the growth in car ownership being accommodated by the issue of additional index marks to the larger local authorities, especially the London County Council, which by 1916 had not only exhausted its original allocation (A) but had also run through combinations beginning with L as far as LR. In 1906 the system was extended to the Isle of Man by an Act of Tynwald. The index mark MN was issued for Manx vehicles and has remained in use as the sole mark for the island since 1906 (except that MAN is used in preference to AMN in marks containing those three letters). The Channel Islands also introduced registration about the same time. In Jersey the letter J was used, followed by a serial number, and in Guernsey a number alone. (For further details of registration in both the Isle of Man and Channel Islands see Appendix 2.) In 1909 the first of a succession of international conventions concerning the passage of motor vehicles between nations was concluded at Paris, which presaged the later use of two-letter index marks beginning with Q in Great Britain for vehicles temporarily imported from abroad; ZZ performed similar duty for vehicles temporarily entering the Irish Free State or Republic of Ireland.

The Roads Act of 1920

The registration system was substantially overhauled by the Roads Act of 1920, the first major measure promoted by the new Ministry of Transport, established under an Act of the previous year in an attempt to place the state's dealings with all forms of transport in the hands of a single department. Thus responsibility for roads, which dominated the work of the Ministry of Transport from its inception, was transferred from the Local Government Board (the rest of whose functions formed the nucleus of the new Ministry of Health), while much less extensive supervisory and regulatory powers over railways and shipping were acquired from the Board of Trade. The Home Office, of course, retained its responsibility for the police, who, since the turn of the century, had been as much involved in motoring matters as the LGB.

The Roads Act confirmed county, county borough and large burgh councils as registration and licensing authorities for vehicles and their drivers, although the Finance Act of the same year changed the financial arrangements concerning excise duty on motor vehicles, which was increased in preference to a tax on petrol. One consequence of this was that henceforth the local authorities acted as agents of the Minister of Transport and records created under the Roads Act have thus been deemed 'public records' in the technical sense defined by the Public Records Act of 1958, whereas those kept under the 1903 Act are records of the registration authorities. The 1920 Act, which came into effect on 1 January 1921, applied, like its predecessor, to the whole of the United Kingdom; supervision of the local authorities was somewhat simplified since the Ministry of Transport, unlike the LGB, was a UK department. On the other hands, given the conditions prevailing in 1920, it was thought prudent to include a clause allowing the minister to administer registration and licensing directly in Ireland, if the local authorities were unable or unwilling to Act. As far as one can judge from limited surviving records, local administration did not break down in Ireland.

As in 1903, detailed arrangements for vehicle registration were contained in an order in council and statutory regulations, issued by the Ministry of Transport in February and March in 1921, which, together with the Act itself, remained the principal legislation until the Vehicles (Excise) Act of 1949 consolidated the law afresh after the

Second World War. The registration provisions of the 1903 Act and orders thereunder were repealed (although other parts of the earlier Act remained on the statute book until repealed by the Road Traffic Act of 1930) and vehicles registered under the 1903 Act were deemed to be registered under that of 1920. Two-letter marks continued to be issued as required, although the reservation of G and V for Scotland was abandoned, leaving only S as a wholly distinctive Scottish mark.

By 1932 the scope for further extension of the two-letter, four-figure system was exhausted and from that year local authorities began to use the more familiar three-figure, three-letter marks. Thus, for example, Hampshire, having reached AA 9999, issued numbers preceded by AAA, BAA, CAA and so on, in blocks of 999 in each case. When this device also failed to keep pace with the growth of car ownership after the Second World War, local authorities were instructed to reverse the order of letters and numbers, which provided sufficient capacity to enable the system to continue into the early 1960s. The practice of adding a suffix letter to six-digit marks was introduced in some registration areas in 1963 and generally the following year. Initially changed on 1 January annually, the suffix letter was later allocated to twelve-month periods beginning on 1 August, at the (far from unanimous) request of the motor trade. By the time most local authorities closed their registers and handed over responsibility to DVLC, the suffix letters had reached M or N.

The legislation of 1920 came into operation shortly before the establishment of Northern Ireland under the Government of Ireland Act, 1920, and the slighly later creation of the Irish Free State. In neither country were arrangements for vehicle registration initially affected, since, under the Government of Ireland Act, all legislation in force in Ireland at the time of the Act's passing remained current until altered by an Act of either the Northern Ireland Parliament or the Dail. Neither made any change to the arrangements of 1920 for some years. As car ownership expanded in Ireland, additional two-letter index marks were drawn from previously unused Z combinations, with local authorities in Northern Ireland using AZ, BZ, CZ etc and those in the Republic ZA, ZB, ZC etc. In practice, only a few of the larger Irish counties and the county boroughs drew on these additional marks, with most of the rural authorities continuing to rely on the I marks originally allocated in 1903 until registration was changed in both parts of Ireland in recent years (see Appendix 1).

Substantial modifications were made to record-keeping under the regulations of 1921. The traditional bound register was retained but was supplemented by a record card for each registration mark and a file for each vehicle. Separate registers ceased to be kept for motorcars and motorcycles (so that it was no longer possible for two vehicles to carry the same mark) but general identification plates were still registered separately, as were imported vehicles assigned Q numbers. The evidence of surviving records indicates that, although the system was supervised by central government, with the local authorities acting as agents of the minister, whose officials issued numerous orders and circulars to local taxation offices, considerable variation developed between local authorities as to how the records were to be kept. Some offices appear to have relied much more on the registration cards than the registers, in which only a minimum of information was entered, and some simply did not complete the forms as fully as others. In general, the detailed descriptions of individual vehicles, including the colour scheme of the bodywork as well as engine capacity and other more mundane details, will not be found in registers kept under the 1920 Act. On the other hand, the registration cards were supposed to include chassis numbers, a unique identifier which can generally be related to manufacturers' records (where they have survived) and which are an important aid to establishing the history (and in some cases the alleged authenticity, antiquity and value) of particular vehicles.

Under the 1921 regulations, like those of 1903, registration authorities were supposed to keep track of changes in ownership, scrapping or export of vehicles registered in their areas. In practice, information of this sort does not seem to have been entered systematically in the registers, although the cards and files may have been marked accordingly. Subsidiary series of forms used for the notification of movements of vehicles between registration authorities have only occasionally survived to reach local record offices. The system had also to accommodate the demand for what used to be called 'personal plates' but are now 'cherished numbers' in the trade, typically those which contain a minimum of letters or numbers, three-letter marks in which the letters spell a word or form the initials of the owner of the vehicle in question, or which for some other reason are deemed to be of special interest. Although such numbers are now marketed commercially by the Department of Transport, in the days of local authority registration they originated simply as marks issued in the ordinary way which were subsequently transferred from one vehicle to another at the request of an owner, in contradistinction to the normal procedure whereby the vehicle retained the same number as it passed from one owner to the next. Because of the extraordinary rise in the value of cherished numbers, allegations of fraudulently compiled plates have been made in recent years, leading on at least one occasion to Crown Court proceedings in which local authority registers have been exhibited. The widespread destruction of such records now makes the detection of fraud of this sort considerably more difficult than it would have been before the setting up of DVLC.

The Vehicle and Driving Licences Act of 1969

The continuing availability of cherished numbers was one of the few aspects of vehicle registration which provoked any discussion when the Vehicle and Driving Licences Bill was introduced into the Commons in November 1968. The bill passed an uneventful second reading one Friday morning, in which few criticisms were made from either side of the House about what was clearly a non-controversial and non-party measure. Indeed, the joint parliamentary secretary to the Ministry of Transport, in moving the second reading, commented on how few representations had been received during the bill's preparation from any part of the extensive and well organised motoring lobby outside Parliament. The Minister announced that the number of local taxation offices would be reduced from 189 to 81, although it would still be possible to pay tax at post offices. A single centralised record of both vehicles and their drivers would be established in a development area in need of new office jobs (i.e. at Swansea, in a region traditionally short of female clerical work), using a (preferably British) computer. At no stage in the debates in either House or in Committee was the question of local authority records and their future raised by either ministers or back-bench speakers. The only issue which aroused real anger was typically English: the question of whether or not residents of the Scilly Isles were liable to pay motor tax to use roads which may or may not have been public highways.

The bill received royal assent in June 1969. In the second reading debate, the minister had expressed the hope that the changeover to a single record would be complete by 1975. In the event, the transitional period extended beyond this and the last agency arrangements between what was by this date the Department of the Environment and local authorities (by now reorganised in both England and Wales and Scotland) were terminated on 31 March 1978.

The Fate of Local Authority Records

What precisely was done with registration records during the lengthy period between 1969 and 1978, or indeed in the following five years up to 1983, when DVLC announced that no further records relating to existing registration marks would be added to their database, remains unclear. In the course of preparing this guide, however, I have spoken to a number of archivists throughout Great Britain who were in post at the time, virtually all of whom feel that large quantities of records were destroyed unnecessarily. Some of these losses may be ascribed to the general problems of local government reorganisation, especially in county boroughs, where in some cases it proved difficult to safeguard records of any kind. In other cases, however, it is clear that destruction followed the issue by the Department of the Environment in 1977 of an instruction to local offices to destroy all vehicle files which had been inactive for more than twelve months. Nothing was said in this circular about the possible transfer of material to local record offices, except in the case of pre-1920 registers and other records, which taxation offices were recommended to offer to 'their local archivist'. Whilst this may have been a reasonable suggestion in England and Wales, it was less helpful in Scotland, where there were very few local archivists in the mid-1970s.

In the case of vehicle files on which there had been recent activity, the DOE evidently instructed local offices to transfer the material to its new Driver & Vehicle Licensing Centre at Swansea. During the 1970s the department maintained at least two intermediate stores elsewhere in South Wales, one at Pontypool (Gwent) and the other at Llandow, a former Second World War RAF station near Bridgend (Mid Glamorgan) later converted into an industrial estate. Since DVLC now hold no local authority registration records at Swansea, and since both the Pontypool and Llandow premises have been given up, the most obvious conclusion is that, once any information deemed to be needed for current administrative use had been extracted from the records for entry on to the DVLC database, the original records were destroyed. No local repository with registration records appears to have received them from DVLC, although there seem to be some instances in which DVLC returned local authority records to police forces. There may also have been cases where records were transferred directly from local taxation offices to the police: it is now difficult to distinguish one process from the other. Nor is it easy to establish what information was transferred from surrendered local authority records to the Swansea computer, since the main source for the database seems to have been the log books issued to vehicle keepers by local authorities, which the public were required to surrender to the department in exchange for a computer-printed Vehicle Registration Document (Form V5, still familiarly called a 'log book'). At any rate, enquiries received today by DVLC concerning the former 'keeper history' of vehicles registered on their computer are answered by the supply of prints from microfilm of local authority log books; the books themselves have presumably been destroyed.

The first formal action by the Public Record Office concerning the fate of local authority registration records in England and Wales was taken in January 1978, when the Liaison Officer issued a circular letter to local repositories drawing attention to the availability of the material and its imminent destruction. By 1978, however, it was a little late still to write that registration was 'being centralised and computerised at Swansea', since the process was largely complete and many records had been destroyed either locally or in South Wales. The PRO circular distinguished between registers kept under the Motor Car Act of 1903, which were the property of the local authorities which originally kept the registers (or their successors under reorganisation), and records (registers, registration cards and files) kept after 1921, which were public records. A small sample of the second category were to be transferred to the PRO but the remainder had not been judged worthy of permanent preservation. 'However', the letter continued, 'those of the period 1921 to 1939 have some interest from the point of view of local history and the historian of the motor industry', and it was therefore proposed to offer them (as well as the 1903-20 registers) to local offices. No explanation was offered as to why records relating to vehicles registered after 1939 (a far higher proportion of which were still in existence than those listed in earlier records) were not also of historical interest, nor does any thought appear to have been given to the needs of owners of surviving older vehicles. It was certainly not the case that all post-1939 records had been retained for current administrative use by the DOE, since large quantities had clearly been destroyed by 1978.

The Liaison Officer invited local repositories to contact taxation offices in their area and take either all or some of the records still at those offices, of which a list was appended to the letter. Formally, any documents acquired in this way would be presented to local repositories under s. 3.6 of the Public Records Act, 1958. The letter concluded by asking local archivists to take action 'as soon as possible, as the Department [of the Environment] wishes to commence the destruction of unwanted records in the very near future'.

There were a number of reasons why the Public Record Office was unable to take action to prevent the loss of registration records until the transfer to DVLC was almost complete. Initially, it took some time after the 1969 Act came into force in 1971 before the status of the post-1920 material as public records was determined. Some further time then elapsed before the PRO and DOE came to the agreement described in the circular of 1978, although the PRO had had informal dealings with interested local record offices, some of which had already acquired registration material. The PRO was in any case unable to issue formal advice to local archivists until it was clear what records the DOE itself required; equally, the issue of the 1978 circular was geared to the closure of local authority taxation departments and could not, from its very nature, be sent until the PRO had obtained from the DOE details of records still at local offices. Once the circular had been issued, the PRO's involvement with the records was very limited. A small representative sample of post-1920 material was taken into the Kew branch of the office and added to the class MT 900 (which is not at present available for public inspection) and in 1988 the department secured the Lord Chancellor's authority for the preservation of the post-1939 as well as the earlier records.

Since the 1958 Public Records Act does not in general apply to Scotland, the Scottish Record Office could not directly follow the procedure adopted by the PRO in England and Wales. The SRO did, however, attempt to discover the present whereabouts of the pre-1920 records of all the Scottish Hregistration authorities, starting with the Edinburgh Licensing Office, which in 1978 had recently arranged for the deposit of the Leith Burgh, Midlothian and West Lothian records in Edinburgh City Archives. Over the country as a whole, however, the survey did not bear a great deal of fruit and it appears that most Scottish registration records which reached archival custody did so through local initiative. It is also clear that a great deal of material was destroyed, either in Scotland or after removal to South Wales (the latter operation itself being a breach of the general rule that the Scottish records of central government departments should be kept in Scotland).

Preserving the Records

Most archivists who discovered, on enquiry at local taxation offices, some or all of the records included in the list circulated by the PRO, took all available material into custody, whether it dated from before 1921, between 1921 and 1939, or after 1939. Only one office (Gloucestershire) appears to have drawn a random sample of post-1921 registration files in preference to keeping the entire series, although the South Yorkshire County Record Office took possession of a large quantity of records which were retained for the time being but have not yet been selected for permanent preservation by the successor office (Sheffield). Similarly, most archive services have listed the documents acquired from taxation offices in a single sequence, ignoring the distinction drawn by the PRO between registers kept under the 1903 Act and post-1921 material.

The bulk of the registration records now in archival custody, whether in England and Wales or Scotland, appear to have been transferred either as result of the PRO's letter of January 1978 or earlier action by the offices themselves. In some cases, however, further transfers have been made since 1978 from police forces, especially of the registration cards kept under the 1921 regulations, since a number of indexes of this sort appear either to have been transferred from taxation offices to the police or returned from DVLC to local forces. Unfortunately, police custody appears to have led to yet further destruction, mainly, it seems, during the 1980s. During the preparation of this book, I was supplied by DVLC with an undated typescript list headed 'Record of Location of Obsolete Files retrieved from LTOs'; subsequent conversation with staff at Swansea established that the word 'Files' in fact meant local taxation office records of any kind. For some counties, this list confirms the complete destruction of records for a particular registration authority, while in others the location given is a local authority archive service. For many areas, however, the location is a police establishment, typically an information room or stolen vehicle department. I drew the attention of a number of archivists (in Scotland as well as England and Wales) to entries on this list which suggested that their local police force might still retain registration records worth safeguarding for future transfer, even if they could not be taken into custody immediately. Only in one case (Essex) did enquiries at police establishments yield any previously unknown material; most commonly the response was a reply from an officer regretting that the records in question had been destroyed some years ago. A particularly unfortunate instance of this was the complete destruction by the West Midlands Constabulary of registration records for the whole of their force area, including some Wolverhampton material which had previously passed to the borough library, from where it was actually returned to the police.

One other location should also be mentioned, the PSV Circle, an omnibus enthusiasts' club, which acquired all the surviving registration cards from the City of Bristol and was claimed (wrongly, it appears) on the DVLC list mentioned in the previous paragraph also to have some Flintshire records. The Bristol material has now been deposited in part in the City Record Office, which is promised the remainder in the near future, while the secretary of the PSV Circle has assured me that his organisation does not hold any other registration records. No evidence has come to light to suggest that other clubs are in possession of registration records.

The Surviving Records

Although it is just possible that more material may still be found, it seems clear that most, if not all, surviving local authority registration records in Great Britain are now in archival custody, generally in county (or approved district) record offices. I have identified nearly one hundred different locations for this material and, inevitably, given the way in which local record keeping operates in Britain, have turned up some oddities which may confuse the searcher. Thus, in

Staffordshire, although county council registration records are at Stafford, those for the former county boroughs of Stoke-on-Trent and Burton-upon-Trent are at Hanley and Burton libraries respectively. The city record office in Chester retains material from the former county borough's local taxation office, whereas fragmentary records from the Swansea office discovered by the city archivist have found their way to the West Glamorgan branch of the county service. Rochdale County Borough records are divided between the Lancashire Record Office at Preston and the Greater Manchester Record Office; some City of Manchester records are at the public library, rather than the record office. For Halifax, some material is at the local library and the remainder at the headquarters of the West Yorkshire Archive Service in Wakefield, where the records of the other former West Riding county boroughs may also be found. In Cleveland, surviving Sunderland records are at the Durham Record Office, rather than that maintained by the county in which Sunderland is situated. These anomalies are simply one aspect of a wider problem unlikely to be resolved until a more carefully worked out system of local record repositories is established in England and Wales. In Scotland there are fewer offices to choose from (and also fewer records) but similar complications have already set in.

A complete list of surviving records for the whole of Great Britain, and also Ireland, follows this introduction and the information set out there need not be repeated here. It is perhaps worth noting, however, that in both England and Wales records kept by county councils tend to be better preserved than those kept by county boroughs and that for several of the largest conurbations (including Birmingham, Manchester and Liverpool as well as London) little or nothing survives. The complete destruction of all records from a county council taxation office seems to be comparatively rare, although there are none for Surrey or Derbyshire; by far the best preserved archive from a shire county is that for Kent. County borough records have generally survived less well and the outstanding collection in this case is that from Doncaster. In Scotland, fewer records of any kind exist but, as in England and Wales, material from the rural counties and smaller burghs tends to have survived better than records kept by Glasgow and Edinburgh.

In most counties, the only material to have reached local archive services are some or all of the registers covering the period from 1903 to the end of local authority registration in a particular area, typically the mid-1970s, or the card index kept from 1921 onwards, or both. In a few counties cards were raised after 1921 for vehicles registered under the 1903 Act. Only in a handful of cases have the individual vehicle files reached archival custody and then rarely with any completeness. A number of offices have registers of driving licences issued under the 1903 Act but there is normally nothing of this sort for the post-1921 period. Registers of trade plates survive rather better, although these are presumably of very limited interest; only Kent seems to have kept registers of vehicles imported from abroad and issued with Q plates. The Kent archive is also distinctive in containing a good range of subsidiary records, including statistical returns and files of Ministry circulars. The equally fine Doncaster records similarly include, besides complete sets of registers and cards, a series of nearly 500 regulations, circulars and other documents received from the Ministry of Transport from 1927 onwards, when the borough became a registration authority. The Glamorgan Record Office has a similar file from the City of Cardiff taxation office of items issued by the Local Government Board under the 1903 Act, which appears to be a unique survival. Such material is of particular importance since there is no corresponding set of instructions issued to local taxation offices among the Ministry of Transport records transferred to the PRO, much less anything from the Local Government Board, although there are some files on various aspects of registration and licensing at Kew, as well as the sample of local records in class MT 900.

Using the Records

Arrangements for access to vehicle registration records now in archival custody vary somewhat across the country, although nowhere do they appear especially onerous. Ever since 1903, public access to information in the registers (although not the registers themselves) has been enshrined in successive statutory orders. Police or Inland Revenue officers were entitled to be supplied with information free of charge; others were to be supplied with the details entered for a particular registration mark on payment of a fee (originally 1s. in 1903), as long as they could show the registration officer that they had 'reasonable cause for requiring such a copy'. This provision was re-enacted in virtually identical terms in later orders and was obviously based on the assumption that the typical enquirer would be an aggrieved motorist, pedestrian or property owner seeking to identify a driver with a view to bringing legal proceedings. The idea of historical research was not conceived of, either in 1903 or later. Nowadays, however, there are few obstacles to their use in this way.

Three possible areas of difficulty suggest themselves. Firstly, a number of offices impose a thirty-year closure period on registration records, possibly because this is normal, in the absence of other arrangements, for public records, possibly because this is the current recommendation of the Association of County Archivists. On the other hand, since post-1921 records have been presented to offices under S.3.6 of the 1958 Act they thereby cease to have the status of public records and there is no obvious justification for such a closure period. General custom and practice would argue against the eccentric imposition of a closure period *greater* than thirty years; conversely, it should be stressed that, in the days of local authority registration, the records were accessible (if not generally open) for all periods. It therefore seems questionable whether, in equity, a record office could refuse to supply information from registration records less than thirty years old, if an enquirer showed reasonable cause for requiring the details relating to a particular mark. To refuse access to the same records to someone interested in more general aspects of motoring history would seem purely cussed. An office could, on the other hand, refuse to produce some material, especially an insecure index of loose cards, on the ground that damage or loss might result.

Secondly, some offices now charge search-fees based on an hourly rate for replying to enquiries by post and at least one charges an admission fee. It might be argued that such offices, if asked for information relating to a particular registration mark, can demand no more than the statutory fee prescribed in the last set of pre-DVLC regulations, which would generally be less than a search fee. A personal caller might also prefer to offer the statutory fee for a copy of an entry in preference for paying for admission to the office where the records are kept. Alternatively, in both cases it could be argued that, since the records are no longer public records, it is for their present owners to make what arrangements they choose for charging fees for access to the information.

Finally, at least two offices have become apprehensive as to the possible abuse of records in their custody following cases which have come to light concerning the sale of fraudulent cherished numbers. The Dumfries Archives Centre, which has registration records for Dumfriesshire and Kirkudbrightshire (those for Wigtownshire are at Stranraer Museum, with no restriction on access), requires a prior written application stating the object of research and the attestation of two referees before it will produce documents or supply information. This precaution, the archivist freely admits, has been taking following a case heard at Liverpool crown court in 1985 in which documents from the office were exhibited. The Sheffield Record Office has inherited similar conditions from the former South Yorkshire office. Here the passage of time has dimmed recollection of the precise reason for requiring a written statement from the searcher as to why he wishes to see registration records (which may be given after arrival in the search-room, rather than in advance), or who originally created the condition, but once again the arrangement probably arose after the cherished number frauds of the 1980s. In fact, anyone proposing to concoct bogus registration marks has no need to choose combinations of letters and numbers whose original issue can be traced in surviving records, since thousands of possibilities, some of considerable commercial value, are readily available incorporating index marks for which all the records have been destroyed, making their authenticity far harder to prove or disprove.

Apart from enquiries from the police or DVLC, and possible undetected visits by purveyors of bogus cherished numbers, most users of registration records in local offices probably fall into one of several fairly obvious categories. The 1903-20 registers offer considerable scope for studies of the local history of car-ownership in the period up to the First World War, when motoring very much a minority pursuit of the rich and most owners whose names and addresses appear in the registers can probably be identified in other sources. Such books also form a major source for the early history of the British motor industry, a period from which relatively few manufacturers' records survive from the numerous small concerns that briefly flourished before the industry was reorganised between the wars. The older records kept under the 1920 Act will also be of value for the general history of the industry, especially for the smaller companies. It is not clear how far genealogists have yet realised the value of registration records for tracing car-ownership amongst recent ancestors, while family historians are perhaps the only group likely to find much of interest in the registers of driving licences kept under the 1903 Act.

For the 1950s and 1960s, the major call on the records will probably be from owners of cars made during this period seeking to trace their history, either out of general interest or because they wish to have the original registration mark restored to their vehicle. In December 1983, DVLC announced that their database was closed to further retrospective entries and that an old car which had been off the road could only be re-registered with its original number if deemed to be of special historical interest, either by virtue of previous ownership or (more justifiably) if it was very rare or represented an important stage in vehicle development. This rule, which has been bitterly contested by owners and clubs, led to the re-registration of vehicles with 'age-related' numbers, i.e. a registration mark which might have been issued by a local authority at about the same time as the vehicle was built but which in practice had not been used. In most cases, this involved using 'spare' numbers from rural counties, especially some of the Scottish counties, with the result that large numbers of classic cars can be seen at rallies bearing marks originally allocated to (but not used by) such thinly populated areas as Kincardineshire or Perthshire, counties for which in both cases all the local authority registration records have been destroyed. Owners who had devoted much time and money to the restoration of their vehicles understandably resented this loss of authenticity, which occasionally reached absurd proportions, as for example with a former Metropolitan Police Wolseley of the 1950s, immaculately restored but bearing a Kinross-shire registration mark.

During 1990 DVLC announced that they were discussing with owners' clubs a relaxation of this rule, with a view to allowing owners to apply for the number originally allocated to a particular vehicle, if they could show what this number was. In the case of owners who had acquired the original local authority log book with a car, this document would presumably constitute sufficient evidence; in other cases it is less clear what would be acceptable to DVLC. Presumably the best evidence would be an entry from a local authority vehicle register, although for many owners such a search would be fruitless, since so many of the records have long been destroyed - at the instigation of DVLC, on the ground that they were no longer of any administrative use. When challenged on this point, DVLC have merely referred owners to the appropriate specialist club for the marque in question. Indeed, so anxious is the department to avoid the complexities of this problem that clubs are to allowed to charge a nominal sum for preparing applications on behalf of members to DVLC for the restoration of an original number (which will then become non-transferable and remain with the vehicle to which it has been assigned). While most clubs will contain a nucleus of members who have spent years investigating the history of a particular marque, possibly with access to any surviving manufacturers' records, and may have compiled a register of all known surviving examples, not even the keenest historian will be able to produce a certified extract from a vehicle register if the document in question has been destroyed. It remains to be seen how DVLC resolve this problem, which is almost entirely of their own making; in the meantime, it seems likely that record offices will see a marked increase in (mostly legitimate!) enquiries concerning vehicle registration records.

Tracing the History of a Vehicle: a Practical Guide

It may be helpful to conclude with a step-by-step guide to tracing the history of a vehicle starting from its registration mark (whether that information is obtained from a plate still attached to the car, an old local authority log-book, a photograph or any other source). In the case of a vehicle whose registration number is not known, the only approach to its history would normally be via the chassis number, about which there is some advice at the end of this section.

The first step is obviously to check the registration mark in the list which follows this introduction, which will supply the name of the local authority to which the mark was allocated. If any records are known to survive, their covering dates will be found in the third column of the table and their present whereabouts in the final column. If there is a dash in the third column and the comment 'Destroyed' or 'Presumed destroyed', that will normally be the end of the matter, unless additional material turns up in the future.

If there are records for the index mark you are interested in, the next step is to contact the location given in the final column, using the list of addresses at the back of the book.

If the location is a local authority record office in England, Scotland or Wales, the best approach is to write (rather than telephone), giving the index mark of the vehicle you are interested in and asking for any details available from their registration records about that mark. Few offices will be able to answer an enquiry on the phone, since the actual records are normally stored in a strong-room some distance away from the search-room in which staff are located. Some offices will take an enquiry over the phone and arrange for the enquirer to ring back the following day; at least two (Dumfries and Sheffield) will definitely not deal with the matter over the phone, for reasons explained above. Some record offices charge a search-fee for answering postal enquiries: these vary considerably across the country, from (at 1991 prices) about £25 an hour in Kent down to £8 in Dorset. Offices which locate an entry in either a register or card index should be able to supply a photocopy, which can, if needed for an application to DVLC, be certified by the archivist as a true copy.

If you wish to visit a record office to search material in person it is always best to ring first and in the case of smaller offices more or less essential, since casual callers cannot always be guaranteed a seat. A prior appointment also saves time, since staff can have at least some of the documents you wish to see ready in the search-room when you arrive. Most offices have a leaflet detailing opening hours and other basic arrangements which they will send to new readers in advance of a visit. It is worth mentioning that most record offices (unlike libraries) are open only during office hours Monday to Friday. An increasing number of offices participate in an identity card system, using a card which secures admission to all the departments concerned. This is surrendered when a document is issued to a reader and returned in exchange for the document at the end of the day. Any participating office will issue one of these cards, for which a photograph may or may not be required. All record offices can supply photocopies of documents to personal callers, although not always on the spot: an order may have to be left and the copies sent on a day or so later. By no means all offices allow readers to take photographs of documents, and anyone wishing to use a camera should ask in advance whether this is permitted.

It should perhaps be stressed that a record office differs fundamentally from a library (even a reference library) in that the documents are not kept on the search-room shelves and readers cannot browse through the material. Each item has to be identified from the appropriate list or index and then requisitioned from the strong-room. This takes time, especially on a first visit, and new visitors to an office should be prepared to learn from the archivist on duty as to what procedures a particular office follows. It is also important to remember that most documents in a record office are unique and irreplaceable and many are fragile. Material must always be handled with great care and notes made only in pencil, not ink. Dictating machines, typewriters or computers should not be taken into a search-room without prior permission.

If the registration mark in which you are interested belongs to an Irish local authority, the next step will depend on whether the county or county borough in question lies in Northern Ireland or the Republic. In Northern Ireland, most surviving records have been centralised at Coleraine, as explained in Appendix 1, and enquiries there should be made by letter. In the Republic, most records are still with the local authorities, often their motor taxation departments. Where an address is given in the list which follows this introduction, enquiries should obviously be made (by letter, rather than phone) as indicated. For a few counties it has proved impossible to secure firm details (or occasionally any information) as to what records survive. In these cases, it is probably worth writing to the motor taxation department of the council in the hope that something may turn up. In both Northern Ireland and the Republic, the actual records, prior to the recent changes described in Appendix 1, are similar to those for British local authorities and their present custodians should be able to supply photocopies.

For Isle of Man and Channel Islands records, the arrangements are set out in Appendix 2. The main point is that Manx records up to 1965 are in archival custody, whereas later material, and all Jersey and Guernsey records, are held by administrative departments with no direct public access. Enquirers should therefore apply by letter rather than phone and be prepared to pay statutory search fees.

Other Sources of Information

In some cases, it may be possible to go from registration records to other material which will provide a fuller history of a particular vehicle.

To take the most obvious case, if the original owner can be identified, it may be possible to trace him in street or trade directories, electoral registers and similar lists of names and addresses available in both libraries and record offices. This may lead to the present whereabouts of the person concerned or his family, who can then be asked for more information. If the vehicle was first registered to a garage, rather than a private owner, it may be possible to trace the firm or its successor. Only exceptionally will sales records have survived but perhaps the principal or one of his longer-serving staff will remember a particular car, especially if it remained locally owned and was maintained by the same garage.

If a vehicle was owned by a company, instead of an individual, it may also be worth tracing the firm (again using directories) and contacting them or any successor. Obviously, the prospects of discovering more about a car will be greater if it was a luxury vehicle bought by a small firm for its managing director than if it was one of thirty bought as a single lot for the sales staff of a much larger concern. Again, it would be surprising if purchase records have survived but, especially in a small company, there may be some personal recollection of a particularly memorable vehicle. In the special case of hearses and other cars used by undertakers, this approach may be particularly profitable, since the vehicles tend to be kept for a long time and, at least until recent years, undertakers were typically small family firms with continuity of ownership.

If a vehicle is known, either from registration records or other sources, to have been owned by a local authority (including the police and fire services) then there may be other possibilities. Both the acquisition and disposal of mayoral cars, especially by small boroughs, would normally require committee approval and here it is worth searching the relevant council minutes, which should now be in the local record office. For more mundane vehicles, the chance of finding details in committee minutes are less good, at any rate from the 1950s onwards, when the use of motor transport by local authorities became commonplace. Similarly, council archives are more likely to contain photographs of mayoral cars than dust-carts, although it is always worth asking a record office if they have any illustrative material. The Middlesbrough Record Office, exceptionally, has a photograph of the first car registered in the borough, acquired with other material from the local taxation office, while Cardiff City

Council retain a good deal of information (including photographs) about the various cars which have borne the registration mark KG 1 and been used by successive lord mayors over more than sixty years.

All this advice is based on the assumption that the car whose history one is trying to trace has never been used by anyone more illustrious than a local mayor. If a car has belonged to someone who is generally well known, then more may be discovered about it from a variety of published and unpublished sources (most obviously newspapers and magazines) which refer to the person, rather than directly to the car. It is clearly impossible to give detailed advice on this subject here and one of the standard local history textbooks should be consulted (see 'Further Reading' below). In the special case of royal cars, it is well known that those owned by the sovereign personally do not carry registration plates, whereas those belonging to other members of the royal family do. All such vehicles, however, are re-registered with a new number and thus a new log book which does not give details of previous ownership, before being disposed of. There are apparently a small number of cars now in private ownership which once belonged to the royal family but this aspect of their history cannot be uncovered directly from registration records.

Finally, there is the question of motor vehicle manufacturers' records and their use in tracing the history of individual cars. Before the First World War, and to a lesser extent between the wars, there were numerous small and medium-sized independent manufacturers in Britain, whose output is now represented by a few surviving examples. Even in the 1950s, there were many more separate companies than there are today. There is no comprehensive guide to the whereabouts of manufacturers' records, large quantities of which must have been lost as a result of mergers and take-overs, as well as the simple demise of some businesses. Even where records have survived, it is by no means certain that the material will identify individual vehicles. Once again, detailed advice on this subject is beyond the scope of this book and anyone tracing the history of a particular car from manufacturers' records would be well advised to contact the appropriate owners' club, which will generally know of any surviving records. (Since most clubs are staffed by voluntary officers, names and addresses change too rapidly for a list to be given here, but such details can be found in (or obtained from) the main monthly classic car magazines.) With any investigation into the history of a particular vehicle, the vital starting-point will normally be a chassis number, unique to the car in question, which can, with luck, be matched against factory records. Indeed, in the absence of a registration number, the chassis number is the only obvious reference, since, where they survive, manufacturers' records should then at least provide a date of building and possibly the name of a customer.

Appendix 1

Vehicle Registration in Ireland since 1921

Since the Roads Act, 1920, came into force shortly before the establishment of Northern Ireland and the Irish Free State, both of whose constitutions provided for the retention of laws enacted by the Imperial Parliament until either the Parliament of Northern Ireland or the Dail decided otherwise, partition did not immediately affect motor vehicle registration in either part of Ireland.

In Northern Ireland, the Roads Act remained the principal statute until the passing of the Vehicles (Excise) Act (NI), 1954, which was in turn replaced by the Vehicles (Excise) Act (NI) 1972, the basis of present-day arrangements. Whereas the 1954 Act merely confirmed existing practice, leaving registration in the hands of the six county councils and two county boroughs (Belfast and Londonderry), that of 1972 removed the administration of the system from the local authorities to the Government of Northern Ireland, a transfer which coincided with a reorganisation of local government in the province that included the abolition of the county councils. The changeover took place on 1 October 1973. As in Great Britain, details of the size, shape, mode of display etc of registration marks are the subject of subsidiary legislation, the current instrument being the Road Vehicles (Registration and Licensing) Regulations (Northern Ireland), 1973.

In principle, all local authority registration records should have passed to the Vehicle Licensing Central Office (County Hall, Castlerock Road, Coleraine BT51 3HS), to whom all enquiries concerning Northern Ireland registration marks should be directed. In practice, some local authority registers are in the Public Record Office of Northern Ireland (66 Balmoral Avenue, Belfast BT9 6NY) or at the Ulster Folk & Transport Museum (Cultra, Holywood BT18 0EU), as detailed in the list of registration marks which follows this introduction.

In the Republic of Ireland (which succeeded the Irish Free State in 1949) registration remains the responsibility of the 26 county councils, plus the four city councils in Dublin, Cork, Limerick and Waterford. The system of registration marks set up by the Acts of 1903 and 1920 remained in use until 1987, when a new scheme was devised incorporating the last two digits of the year in which a vehicle was first registered.

Most registration records are still in the hands of the motor taxation departments of local authorities, although in Dublin and a few other towns some books have been transferred to archival (or library) custody. Details of the whereabouts of the records for all 30 authorities are given in the list below, except in a few cases where it has proved impossible to secure a reply from the county council in question. The replies given by most local authorities indicate that they hold records from whatever date (1903 or later) they first survive up to the present. Those in the Dublin City Archives, however, extend only to 1954, later registers having been transferred to the Department of the Environment at Shannon, Co. Clare, where the information is being entered on computer. It has proved impossible to establish whether the post-1955 records of other registration authorities have been similarly transferred or whether the records that have gone to Shannon are to be preserved there, returned to the local authorities or destroyed.

Appendix 2

Vehicle Registration in the Isle of Man and Channel Islands

Vehicle registration was introduced into the Isle of Man by an Act of Tynwald of 1905, the Highways Act Amendment Act, and the registers begin in January 1906. There have been a number of later statutes but the system of registration, using MN as the index mark, has not basically altered since its inception. The registers themselves, a single series covering the whole island, are at the Manx Museum, Douglas, until 1965, thereafter at the Vehicle Licensing Section of the Treasury (Government Offices, Buck's Road, Douglas).

Statutory control of motor vehicles on Guernsey began with a provisional ordinance of 1903, made permanent in 1908, which provided for owners to notify the constables of St Peter Port of the number of vehicles owned and to pay £1 tax per vehicle. In 1913 Guernsey became party to the international convention governing the passage of vehicles abroad and in 1915 a comprehensive law relating to registration, taxation and the licensing of drivers was enacted by the States. This was replaced in 1926 by a law which, with amendments, remains the basis of present-day arrangements. Apart from minor variations for official cars and trade plates, Guernsey's registration system relies simply on a serial number, which had reached 56000 by 1988. Vehicles used on Alderney are registered with a number prefaced by the letters AY.

Registration records for Guernsey and Alderney are in the custody of the Vehicle Registration and Licensing Department of the States Board of Administration, PO Box 145, Guernsey, Channel Islands. They are not open to the public but the department will answer enquiries.

Registration on Jersey was introduced in 1915 under a law enacted by the States the previous year and the principal statute in force today dates from 1957. The registration mark consists of the letter J followed by a five-figure serial number. The records, which date from 1915, are in the custody of the Motor Taxation Department of the States Treasury, Cyril le Marquand House, The Parade, St Helier,

Jersey, Channel Islands. They are not open to the public but again, on payment of a fee, the department will supply information to enquirers if a sufficient reason is given.

Further Reading

William Plowden, *The Motor Car and Politics, 1896-1970* (Bodley Head, 1971).
An excellent general account, with full references and bibliography; almost the only historical study of the Ministry of Transport.

R.G.A. Chesterman, *Laughter in the House. Local Taxation and the Motor Car in Cheshire, 1888-1978* (Cheshire County Council, 1978).
A thorough local study (the only one of its kind), prefaced by a good outline of the legislation relating to motor vehicle taxation.

Kitchin's Road Transport Law (ed. James Duckworth, 26th edition, Butterworths, 1988).
Chapter 19 sets out the law under the 1969 Act and later legislation.

John Shearman, *'The Archives of Motoring'*, Archives, II (1956), 369-81.
A pioneer attempt to describe sources for motoring history, although omitting to mention registration records.

Richard Storey, *'Motor Vehicle Registers'*, Archives, VII (1965), 91-2.
The first article to draw attention to the historical interest of registration records.

'Nottinghamshire Register of Motor Cars and Motor Cycles, 1903', Thoroton Society of Nottinghamshire Record Series, XXI (1962), 65-79.
The only published example of an early register.

Baron F. Duckham, *'Early Motor Vehicle Licence Records and the Local Historian'*, The Local Historian, XVII (1986-7), 351-7.
Illustrates use of registration records for the history of car ownership before 1920 by a case-study of three rural Welsh counties. Fails to appreciate how much material has been destroyed.

P. Riden, *Local History. A Handbook for Beginners* (B.T. Batsford, Revised reprint, 1989).
The only up-to-date introductory textbook for local historians in England and Wales.

W.B. Stephens, *Sources for English Local History* (Cambridge University Press, 1981).
The standard general guide to sources of all kinds, with a short section on transport.

P. Riden, *Record Sources for Local History* (B.T. Batsford, 1987).
Detailed guide to archival sources in both the Public Record Office and local repositories.

Motor Vehicle Index Marks and Surviving Registers

The following table lists every index mark used in Great Britain, Ireland and the Isle of Man since 1903, together with the name of the local authority to which it was allocated. The letter 'B' after the name of a town indicates that it was a county borough or large burgh. The two right-hand columns list the covering dates of any registration records known to survive for each mark and their present location. An asterisk refers to the notes at the end of the table. For the full address and telephone number of each of the locations in the fourth column see the list at the back of the booklet. Where records are divided between two different places in the same town, the locations have been distinguished as (e.g.) Manchester A and Manchester B. In general, the table is a list of vehicle *registers;* where the only surviving records are registration cards or files this is made clear in the notes.

Index Mark	Registration Authority	Surviving Registers Dates	Location
A	London	–	Destroyed
AA	Hampshire	1904–13	Winchester
AB	Worcestershire	1903–21	Worcester
AC	Warwickshire	1903–75	Warwick
AD	Gloucestershire	1903–74*	Gloucester
AE	Bristol B	1904–40*	Bristol
AF	Cornwall	1903–20	Truro
AG	Ayrshire	–	Presumed destroyed
AH	Norfolk	1904–20	Norwich
AI	Meath	1904– *	Navan
AJ	Yorkshire NR	1903–12	Northallerton
AK	Bradford B	1903–77*	Wakefield
AL	Nottinghamshire	1903–55*	Nottingham
AM	Wiltshire	1903–64	Trowbridge
AN	West Ham B	–	Presumed destroyed
AO	Cumberland	1903–74	Carlisle
AP	Sussex (East)	1903–74	Lewes
AR	Hertfordshire	1903–77	Hertford

AS	Nairnshire	–	Presumed destroyed
AT	Kingston-upon-Hull B	1904–74*	Hull
AU	Nottingham B	–	Presumed destroyed
AV	Aberdeenshire	–	Presumed destroyed
AW	Salop	1921–72*	Shrewsbury
AX	Monmouthshire	1904–74	Cwmbran
AY	Leicestershire	1903–22	Leicester
AZ	Belfast B	*	
B	Lancashire	1921–41	Preston
BA	Salford B	1904–70*	Salford
BB	Newcastle-upon-Tyne B	–	Presumed destroyed
BC	Leicester B	–	Destroyed
BD	Northamptonshire	1903–78*	Northampton
BE	Lincolnshire (Lindsey)	1904–74*	Lincoln
BF	Dorsetshire	1903–04*	Dorchester
BG	Birkenhead B	–	Presumed destroyed
BH	Buckinghamshire	1903–74	Aylesbury
BI	Monaghan	1933– *	Monaghan
BJ	Suffolk (East)	1903–23*	Ipswich
BK	Portsmouth B	–	Presumed destroyed
BL	Berkshire	1904–20	Reading
BM	Bedfordshire	1903–64	Bedford
BN	Bolton B	1903–20	Bolton
BO	Cardiff B	1922–29	Cardiff
BP	Sussex (West)	1903–20*	Chichester
BR	Sunderland B	1921–33	Durham
BS	Orkney	1904–76	Kirkwall
BT	Yorkshire (ER)	1905–76	Beverley
BU	Oldham B	1903–20	Oldham
		1926–30*	Manchester A
BV	Blackburn B	1954–74	Preston
BW	Oxfordshire	1903–74	Oxford
BX	Carmarthenshire	1907–77	Carmarthen
BY	Croydon B	–	Presumed destroyed
BZ	Down	*	
C	Yorkshire (WR)	*	
CA	Denbighshire	1903–76*	Ruthin
CB	Blackburn B	1954–74	Preston

CC	Caernarvonshire	1904–77	Caernarfon
CD	Brighton B	1904–77	Lewes
CE	Cambridgeshire	*	
CF	Suffolk (West)	–	Presumed destroyed
CG	Hampshire	–	Presumed destroyed
CH	Derby B	1903–47*	Matlock
CI	Leix Laoighis	1940–	Portlaoise
CJ	Herefordshire	1904–74*	Hereford
CK	Preston B	1904–39	Preston
CL	Norwich B	–	Destroyed
CM	Birkenhead B	–	Presumed destroyed
CN	Gateshead B	–	Presumed destroyed
CO	Plymouth B	1921–74*	Plymouth
CP	Halifax B	1904–11	Halifax
		1921–31*	Halifax
		1921–77*	Wakefield
CR	Southampton B	1903–19*	Southampton
CS	Ayrshire	–	Presumed destroyed
CT	Lincolnshire (Kesteven)	1923–74*	Lincoln
CU	South Shields B	–	Presumed destroyed
CV	Cornwall	–	Destroyed
CW	Burnley B	1904–52	Preston
CX	Huddersfield B	1921–77*	Wakefield
CY	Swansea B	1921–29	Swansea
CZ	Belfast B	*	
D	Kent	1903–13	Maidstone
DA	Wolverhampton B	1925–56*	Wolverhampton
DB	Stockport B	1932–68*	Manchester A
DC	Middlesbrough B	1904–19	Middlesbrough
		1937–47	Middlesbrough
DD	Gloucestershire	1921–74*	Gloucester
DE	Pembrokeshire	1903–74	Haverfordwest
DF	Gloucestershire	1926–74*	Gloucester
DG	Gloucestershire	1929–74*	Gloucester
DH	Walsall B	1904–57*	Walsall
DI	Roscommon	1930–	Roscommon
DJ	St Helens B	1904–20	St Helens
DK	Rochdale B	1919–21	Preston
		1927–75	Manchester A

DL	Isle of Wight	–	Destroyed
DM	Flintshire	1903–36	Hawarden
DN	York B	1948–73	York
DO	Lincolnshire (Holland)	1904–20	Lincoln
		1932–74*	Lincoln
DP	Reading B	–	Destroyed
DR	Plymouth B	1926–74*	Plymouth
DS	Peeblesshire	–	Presumed destroyed
DT	Doncaster B	1927–74	Doncaster
DU	Coventry B	1921–63*	Coventry
DV	Devonshire	–	Presumed destroyed
DW	Newport (Mon.)	1914–74	Cwmbran
DX	Ipswich B	1904–50	Ipswich
DY	Hastings B	1903–74	Lewes
DZ	Antrim	*	
E	Staffordshire	1920–25	Stafford
EA	West Bromwich B	1925–27	Smethwick
EB	Isle of Ely	1903–66	Cambridge
EC	Westmorland	1904–09	Kendal
		1925–74*	Kendal
ED	Warrington B	1922–74	Chester A
EE	Grimsby B	1904–74	Grimsby
EF	West Hartlepool B	1903–64	Middlesbrough
EG	Soke of Peterborough	1931–74	Huntingdon
EH	Stoke-on-Trent B	1904–20	Hanley
EI	Sligo	1903–	Sligo
EJ	Cardiganshire	1903–73	Aberystwyth
EK	Wigan B	1932–78*	Leigh
EL	Bournemouth B	1903–77	Dorchester
EM	Bootle B	–	Presumed destroyed
EN	Bury B	1904–75*	Manchester A
EO	Barrow-in-Furness B	1904–64	Barrow-in-Furness
EP	Montgomeryshire	1903–74*	Llandrindod Wells
ER	Cambridgeshire	1965–66*	Cambridge
ES	Perthshire	1909–10	Dundee
ET	Rotherham B	1903–25	Sheffield
		1936–74	Sheffield
EU	Brecknockshire	1903–74	Llandrindod Wells
EV	Essex	1931–45	Chelmsford

EW	Huntingdonshire	1921–75*	Huntingdon
EX	Great Yarmouth B	1921–54	Norwich
EY	Anglesey	1903–74	Llangefni
EZ	Belfast B	*	
F	Essex	1904–20	Chelmsford
FA	Burton-upon-Trent B	1903–22	Burton-upon-Trent
FB	Bath B	–	Presumed destroyed
FC	Oxford B	1922–74	Oxford
FD	Dudley B	1903–74	Dudley
FE	Lincoln B	1903–20*	Lincoln
FF	Merionethshire	1921–74	Dolgellau
FH	Gloucester B	1910–19*	Gloucester
FI	Tipperary (NR)	–	No information
FJ	Exeter B	1903–20	Exeter
FK	Worcester B	1903–42	Worcester
FL	Soke of Peterborough	1903–75	Huntingdon
FM	Chester B	1903–78	Chester B
FN	Canterbury B	1904–29	Canterbury
FO	Radnorshire	1903–74	Llandrindod Wells
FP	Rutlandshire	1903–60	Leicester
FR	Blackpool B	1920–74	Preston
FS	Edinburgh B	–	Presumed destroyed
FT	Tynemouth B	–	Presumed destroyed
FU	Lincolnshire (Lindsey)	*	Lincoln
FV	Blackpool B	1920–74	Preston
FW	Lincolnshire (Lindsey)	*	Presumed destroyed
FX	Dorsetshire	1903–74*	Dorchester
FY	Southport B	–	Presumed destroyed
FZ	Belfast B	*	
G	Glasgow B	–	Presumed destroyed
GA	Glasgow B	–	Presumed destroyed
GB	Glasgow B	–	Presumed destroyed
GC	London	–	Destroyed
GD	Glasgow B	–	Presumed destroyed
GE	Glasgow B	–	Presumed destroyed
GF	London	–	Destroyed
GG	Glasgow B	–	Presumed destroyed
GH	London	–	Destroyed

GJ	London	–	Destroyed
GK	London	–	Destroyed
GL	Bath B	–	Presumed destroyed
GM	Motherwell & Wishaw B	–	Presumed destroyed
GN	London	–	Destroyed
GO	London	–	Destroyed
GP	London	–	Destroyed
GR	Sunderland B	1955–65*	Durham
GS	Perthshire	–	Presumed destroyed
GT	London	–	Destroyed
GU	London	–	Destroyed
GV	Suffolk (West)	1930–46*	Bury St Edmunds
GW	London	–	Destroyed
GX	London	–	Destroyed
GY	London	–	Destroyed
GZ	Belfast B	*	
H	Middlesex	–	Destroyed
HA	Smethwick B	–	Presumed destroyed
HB	Merthyr Tydfil B	–	Presumed destroyed
HC	Eastbourne B	1927–74	Lewes
HD	Dewsbury B	1913–77*	Wakefield
HE	Barnsley B	1913–76	Sheffield
HF	Wallasey B	1913–15	Birkenhead
HG	Burnley B	1925–52	Preston
HH	Carlisle B	1922–74	Carlisle
HI	Tipperary (SR)	–	No information
HJ	Southend B	1914–46	Southend
HK	Essex	1915–45	Chelmsford
HL	Wakefield B	1943–76	Wakefield
HM	East Ham B	–	Presumed destroyed
HN	Darlington B	1915–74	Darlington
HO	Hampshire	1912	Winchester
HP	Coventry B	1921–63*	Coventry
HR	Wiltshire	1919–64	Trowbridge
HS	Renfrewshire	1903–49	Glasgow
HT	Bristol B	1904–40*	Bristol
HU	Bristol B	1904–40*	Bristol
HV	East Ham B	–	Presumed destroyed
HW	Bristol B	1904–40*	Bristol

HX	Middlesex	–	Destroyed
HY	Bristol B	1904–40*	Bristol
HZ	Tyrone	*	
IA	Antrim	1903–20*	Holywood
IB	Armagh	1925–27	Belfast
		1952–57*	Belfast
IC	Carlow	–	No information
ID	Cavan	–	Destroyed
IE	Clare	1973–	Ennis
IF	Cork (County)	–	No information
IH	Donegal	1903– *	Letterkenny
IJ	Down	*	
IK	Dublin (County)	1927–54	Dublin
IL	Fermanagh	*	
IM	Galway	1920–	Galway
IN	Kerry	1903–	Tralee
IO	Kildare	1917–53*	Newbridge
IP	Kilkenny	1903– *	Kilkenny
IR	Offaly	1904–23	Tullamore
		1945– *	Tullamore
IT	Leitrim	1950–	Carrick on Shannon
IU	Limerick	1903–23*	Limerick
IW	Londonderry	*	
IX	Longford	–	No information
IY	Louth	1921–	Dundalk
IZ	Mayo	1904–	Castlebar
J	Durham (County)	–	Presumed destroyed
JA	Stockport B	1932–68*	Manchester A
JB	Berkshire	–	Destroyed
JC	Caernarvonshire	1952–77*	Caernarfon
JD	West Ham B	–	Presumed destroyed
JE	Isle of Ely	1933–64	Cambridge
JF	Leicester B	–	Destroyed
JG	Canterbury B	1904–29	Canterbury
JH	Hertfordshire	1934–77	Hertford
JI	Tyrone	*	
JJ	London	–	Destroyed
JK	Eastbourne B	1927–74	Lewes

JL	Lincolnshire (Holland)	1904–20	Lincoln
		1932–74*	Lincoln
JM	Westmorland	1925–74*	Kendal
JN	Southend B	1922–46	Southend
JO	Oxford B	1930–74	Oxford
JP	Wigan B	1934–78*	Leigh
JR	Northumberland	1904–61	Newcastle
JS	Ross & Cromarty	1974	Inverness
JT	Dorsetshire	1933–75	Dorchester
JU	Leicestershire	1932–36	Leicester
JV	Grimsby B	1904–74	Grimsby
JW	Wolverhampton B	1925–56*	Wolverhampton
JX	Halifax B	1935–57*	Halifax
		1933–77*	Wakefield
JY	Plymouth B	1932–74	Plymouth
JZ	Down	*	
K	Liverpool B	–	Presumed destroyed
KA	Liverpool B	–	Presumed destroyed
KB	Liverpool B	–	Presumed destroyed
KC	Liverpool B	–	Presumed destroyed
KD	Liverpool B	–	Presumed destroyed
KE	Kent	1920–74	Maidstone
KF	Liverpool B	–	Presumed destroyed
KG	Cardiff B	1930–37	Cardiff
KH	Kingston-upon-Hull B	1904–74*	Hull
KI	Waterford	1903– *	Waterford
KJ	Kent	1931–74	Maidstone
KL	Kent	1924–74	Maidstone
KK	Kent	1922–74	Maidstone
KL	Kent	1924–74	Maidstone
KM	Kent	1925–74	Maidstone
KN	Kent	1917–74	Maidstone
KO	Kent	1927–74	Maidstone
KP	Kent	1928–74	Maidstone
KR	Kent	1929–74	Maidstone
KS	Roxburghshire	–	Presumed destroyed
KT	Kent	1913–74	Maidstone
KU	Bradford B	1921–77*	Wakefield
KV	Coventry B	1921–63*	Coventry

KW	Bradford B	1921–77*	Wakefield
KX	Buckinghamshire	1927–74	Aylesbury
KY	Bradford B	1921–77*	Wakefield
KZ	Antrim	*	
L	Glamorganshire	1903–20	Cardiff
LA	London	–	Destroyed
LB	London	–	Destroyed
LC	London	–	Destroyed
LD	London	–	Destroyed
LE	London	–	Destroyed
LF	London	–	Destroyed
LG	Cheshire	1928–74	Chester A
LH	London	–	Destroyed
LI	Westmeath	*	
LJ	Bournemouth B	1929–77	Dorchester
LK	London	–	Destroyed
LL	London	–	Destroyed
LM	London	–	Destroyed
LN	London	–	Destroyed
LO	London	–	Destroyed
LP	London	–	Destroyed
LR	London	–	Destroyed
LS	Selkirkshire	–	Presumed destroyed
LT	London	1917–19*	London
LU	London	–	Destroyed
LV	Liverpool B	–	Presumed destroyed
LW	London	–	Destroyed
LX	London	–	Destroyed
LY	London	–	Destroyed
LZ	Armagh	*	
M	Cheshire	1903–19	Chester A
MA	Cheshire	1919–74	Chester A
MB	Cheshire	1922–74	Chester A
MC	Middlesex	–	Destroyed
MD	Middlesex	–	Destroyed
ME	Middlesex	–	Destroyed
MF	Middlesex	–	Destroyed
MG	Middlesex	–	Destroyed

MH	Middlesex	–	Destroyed
MI	Wexford	1921– *	Wexford
MJ	Bedfordshire	1932–64	Bedford
MK	Middlesex	–	Destroyed
ML	Middlesex	–	Destroyed
MM	Middlesex	–	Destroyed
MN	Isle of Man	1906–65*	Douglas
MO	Berkshire	1922–24	Reading
MP	Middlesex	–	Destroyed
MR	Wiltshire	1924–64	Trowbridge
MS	Stirlingshire	1903–21	Stirling
MT	Middlesex	–	Destroyed
MU	Middlesex	–	Destroyed
MV	Middlesex	–	Destroyed
MW	Wiltshire	1927–64	Trowbridge
MX	Middlesex	–	Destroyed
MY	Middlesex	–	Destroyed
MZ	Belfast B	*	
N	Manchester B	–	Presumed destroyed
NA	Manchester B	1968–74*	Manchester B
NB	Manchester B	1968–74*	Manchester B
NC	Manchester B	1968–74*	Manchester B
ND	Manchester B	1968–74*	Manchester B
NE	Manchester B	1968–74*	Manchester B
NF	Manchester B	1968–84*	Manchester B
NG	Norfolk	–	Presumed destroyed
NH	Northampton B	–	Presumed destroyed
NI	Wicklow	1922–	Wicklow
NJ	Sussex (East)	1933–76	Lewes
NK	Hertfordshire	1934–77	Hertford
NL	Northumberland	1904–61	Newcastle
NM	Bedfordshire	1920–64	Bedford
NN	Nottinghamshire	1921–55*	Nottingham
NO	Essex	1921–45	Chelmsford
NP	Worcestershire	1921–27	Worcester
NR	Leicestershire	1921–27	Leicester
NS	Sutherlandshire	–	Presumed destroyed
NT	Salop	1921–72*	Shrewsbury
NU	Derbyshire	–	Presumed destroyed

NV	Northamptonshire	1924–78*	Northampton
NW	Leeds B	1921–77*	Wakefield
NX	Warwickshire	1921–75	Warwick
NY	Glamorganshire	–	Presumed destroyed
NZ	Londonderry	*	
O	Birmingham B	*	Birmingham
OA	Birmingham B	–	Destroyed
OB	Birmingham B	–	Destroyed
OC	Birmingham B	–	Destroyed
OD	Devonshire	–	Presumed destroyed
OE	Birmingham B	–	Destroyed
OF	Birmingham B	–	Destroyed
OG	Birmingham B	–	Destroyed
OH	Birmingham B	–	Destroyed
OI	Belfast B	*	
OJ	Birmingham B	–	Destroyed
OK	Birmingham B	–	Destroyed
OL	Birmingham B	–	Destroyed
OM	Birmingham B	–	Destroyed
ON	Birmingham B	–	Destroyed
OP	Birmingham B	–	Destroyed
OR	Hampshire	1924–26	Winchester
OS	Wigtownshire	1904–22	Stranraer
OT	Hampshire	1925–28	Winchester
OU	Hampshire	1928–31	Winchester
OV	Birmingham B	–	Destroyed
OW	Southampton B	*	Southampton
OX	Birmingham B	–	Destroyed
OY	Croydon B	–	Presumed destroyed
OZ	Belfast B	*	
P	Surrey	–	Presumed destroyed
PA	Surrey	–	Presumed destroyed
PB	Surrey	–	Presumed destroyed
PC	Surrey	–	Presumed destroyed
PD	Surrey	–	Presumed destroyed
PE	Surrey	–	Presumed destroyed
PF	Surrey	–	Presumed destroyed

PG	Surrey	–	Presumed destroyed
PH	Surrey	–	Presumed destroyed
PI	Cork B	–	No information
PJ	Surrey	–	Presumed destroyed
PK	Surrey	–	Presumed destroyed
PL	Surrey	–	Presumed destroyed
PM	Sussex (East)	1923–76	Lewes
PN	Sussex (East)	1927–74	Lewes
PO	Sussex (West)	*	
PP	Buckinghamshire	1927–74	Aylesbury
PR	Dorsetshire	1923–75	Dorchester
PS	Shetland	1904–72*	Lerwick
PT	Durham (County)	1922–62	Durham
PU	Essex	1921–45	Chelmsford
PV	Ipswich B	1904–50	Ipswich
PW	Norfolk	–	Presumed destroyed
PX	Sussex (West)	*	
PY	Yorkshire (NR)	–	Presumed destroyed
PZ	Belfast B	*	
R	Derbyshire	–	Presumed destroyed
RA	Derbyshire	–	Presumed destroyed
RB	Derbyshire	–	Presumed destroyed
RC	Derby B	1933–47*	Matlock
RD	Reading B	–	Destroyed
RE	Staffordshire	1921–47	Stafford
RF	Staffordshire	1925–38	Stafford
RG	Aberdeen B	–	Presumed destroyed
RH	Kingston-upon-Hull B	1908–74*	Hull
RI	Dublin B	1927–54	Dublin
RJ	Salford B	1931–69*	Salford
RK	Croydon B	–	Presumed destroyed
RL	Cornwall	–	Destroyed
RM	Cumberland	1903–74	Carlisle
RN	Preston B	1904–39	Preston
RO	Hertfordshire	1934–77	Hertford
RP	Northamptonshire	1924–78*	Northampton
RR	Nottinghamshire	1921–55*	Nottingham
RS	Aberdeen B	–	Presumed destroyed
RT	Suffolk (East)	*	Ipswich

RU	Bournemouth B	1926–76	Dorchester
RV	Portsmouth B	–	Presumed destroyed
RW	Coventry B	1924–63*	Coventry
RX	Berkshire	–	Destroyed
RY	Leicester B	–	Destroyed
RZ	Antrim	*	
S	Edinburgh B	–	Presumed destroyed
SA	Aberdeenshire	–	Presumed destroyed
SB	Argyllshire	1903–20	Lochgilphead
SC	Edinburgh B	–	Presumed destroyed
SD	Ayrshire	–	Presumed destroyed
SE	Banffshire	1903–38*	Forres
SF	Edinburgh B	–	Presumed destroyed
SG	Edinburgh B	–	Presumed destroyed
SH	Berwickshire	–	Presumed destroyed
SJ	Buteshire	1903–21	Glasgow
SK	Caithness-shire	–	Presumed destroyed
SL	Clackmannanshire	–	Presumed destroyed
SM	Dumfriesshire	1903–70*	Dumfries
SN	Dunbartonshire	–	Presumed destroyed
SO	Morayshire	1903–46*	Forres
SP	Fifeshire	–	Presumed destroyed
SR	Angus	1903–74	Dundee
SS	East Lothian	–	Presumed destroyed
ST	Inverness-shire	1903–75	Inverness
SU	Kincardineshire	–	Presumed destroyed
SV	Kinross-shire	1904–53	Dundee
SW	Kirkudbrightshire	1903–76*	Dumfries
SX	Linlithgow	1904–21	Edinburgh
		1934–59	Edinburgh
SY	Midlothian	*	
SZ	Down	*	
T	Devonshire	1903–20	Exeter
TA	Devonshire	1920–22	Exeter
TB	Lancashire	1921–41	Preston
TC	Lancashire	1921–41	Preston
TD	Lancashire	1921–41	Preston

TE	Lancashire	1921–41	Preston
TF	Lancashire	1921–41	Preston
TG	Glamorganshire	–	Presumed destroyed
TH	Carmarthenshire	1929–77	Carmarthen
TI	Limerick B	1904– *	Limerick
TJ	Lancashire	1921–41	Preston
TK	Dorsetshire	1927–71	Dorchester
TL	Lincolnshire (Kesteven)	1923–74*	Lincoln
TM	Bedfordshire	1927–62	Bedford
TN	Newcastle-upon-Tyne B	–	Presumed destroyed
TO	Nottingham B	–	Presumed destroyed
TP	Portsmouth B	–	Presumed destroyed
TR	Southampton B	*	Southampton
TS	Dundee B	1904–81	Dundee
TT	Devonshire	–	Presumed destroyed
TU	Cheshire	1925–74	Chester A
TV	Nottingham B	–	Presumed destroyed
TW	Essex	1925–45	Chelmsford
TX	Glamorganshire	–	Presumed destroyed
TY	Northumberland	1904–61	Newcastle
TZ	Belfast B	*	
U	Leeds B	1921–77*	Wakefield
UA	Leeds B	1921–77*	Wakefield
UB	Leeds B	1921–77*	Wakefield
UC	London	–	Destroyed
UD	Oxfordshire	1927–74	Oxford
UE	Warwickshire	1925–75	Warwick
UF	Brighton B	1925–78	Lewes
UG	Leeds B	1932–46*	Wakefield
UH	Cardiff B	1925–37	Cardiff
UI	Londonderry B	*	
UJ	Salop	1921–72*	Shrewsbury
UK	Wolverhampton B	1925–56*	Wolverhampton
UL	London	–	Destroyed
UM	Leeds B	1921–77*	Wakefield
UN	Denbighshire	1921–76*	Ruthin
UO	Devonshire	–	Presumed destroyed
UP	Durham (County)	1927–60	Durham
UR	Hertfordshire	1934–77	Hertford

US	Glasgow B	–	Presumed destroyed
UT	Leicestershire	1927–32	Leicester
UU	London	–	Destroyed
UV	London	–	Destroyed
UW	London	–	Destroyed
UX	Salop	1921–72*	Shrewsbury
UY	Worcestershire	1926–31	Worcester
UZ	Belfast B	*	
V	Lanarkshire	–	Presumed destroyed
VA	Lanarkshire	–	Presumed destroyed
VB	Croydon B	–	Presumed destroyed
VC	Coventry B	1929–63*	Coventry
VD	Lanarkshire	–	Presumed destroyed
VE	Cambridgeshire	*	
VF	Norfolk	–	Presumed destroyed
VG	Norwich B	–	Destroyed
VH	Huddersfield B	1921–77*	Wakefield
VJ	Herefordshire	1921–74*	Hereford
VK	Newcastle-upon-Tyne B	–	Presumed destroyed
VL	Lincoln B	–	Presumed destroyed
VM	Manchester B	1968–74*	Manchester B
VN	Yorkshire NR	–	Presumed destroyed
VO	Nottinghamshire	1921–55*	Nottingham
VP	Birmingham B	–	Destroyed
VR	Manchester B	1968–74*	Manchester B
VS	Greenock B	–	Presumed destroyed
VT	Stoke-on-Trent B	1904–20	Hanley
VU	Manchester B	1968–74*	Manchester B
VV	Northampton B	–	Presumed destroyed
VW	Essex	1927–45	Chelmsford
VX	Essex	1929–45	Chelmsford
VY	York B	1948–73	York
VZ	Tyrone	*	
W	Sheffield B	1903–05	Sheffield
WA	Sheffield B	1931–61*	Sheffield
WB	Sheffield B	1931–61*	Sheffield
WD	Warwickshire	1930–75	Warwick
WE	Sheffield B	1931–61*	Sheffield

WF	Yorkshire (ER)	1932–76	Beverley
WG	Stirlingshire	–	Presumed destroyed
WH	Bolton B	–	Presumed destroyed
WI	Waterford B	1903– *	Waterford
WJ	Sheffield B	1931–71*	Sheffield
WK	Coventry B	1926–63*	Coventry
WL	Oxford B	1926–74	Oxford
WM	Southport B	–	Presumed destroyed
WN	Swansea B	–	Destroyed
WO	Monmouthshire	1927–74	Cwmbran
WP	Worcestershire	1931–35	Worcester
WR	Yorkshire (WR)	–	Presumed destroyed
WS	Leith B	1903–20*	Edinburgh
WT	Yorkshire (WR)	–	Presumed destroyed
WU	Yorkshire (WR)	–	Presumed destroyed
WV	Wiltshire	1931–64	Trowbridge
WW	Yorkshire (WR)	–	Presumed destroyed
WX	Yorkshire (WR)	–	Presumed destroyed
WY	Yorkshire (WR)	–	Presumed destroyed
WZ	Belfast B	*	
X	Northumberland	1903–21*	Newcastle
XA	London	–	Destroyed
XB	London	–	Destroyed
XC	London	–	Destroyed
XD	London	–	Destroyed
XE	London	–	Destroyed
XF	London	–	Destroyed
XG	Middlesbrough B	1937–47	Middlesbrough
XH	London	–	Destroyed
XI	Belfast B	*	
XJ	Manchester B	1968–74*	Manchester B
XK	London	–	Destroyed
XL	London	–	Destroyed
XM	London	–	Destroyed
XN	London	–	Destroyed
XO	London	–	Destroyed
XP	London	–	Destroyed
XR	London	–	Destroyed
XS	Paisley B	–	Presumed destroyed

XT	London	–	Destroyed
XU	London	–	Destroyed
XV	London	–	Destroyed
XW	London	–	Destroyed
XX	London	–	Destroyed
XY	London	–	Destroyed
XZ	Armagh	*	
Y	Somerset	1903–20	Taunton
YA	Somerset	1921–74	Taunton
YB	Somerset	1924–74	Taunton
YC	Somerset	1927–74	Taunton
YD	Somerset	1931–74	Taunton
YE	London	–	Destroyed
YF	London	–	Destroyed
YG	Yorkshire (WR)	–	Presumed destroyed
YH	London	–	Destroyed
YI	Dublin B	1927–54	Dublin
YJ	Dundee B	1932–48	Dundee
YK	London	–	Destroyed
YL	London	–	Destroyed
YM	London	–	Destroyed
YN	London	–	Destroyed
YO	London	–	Destroyed
YP	London	–	Destroyed
YR	London	–	Destroyed
YS	Glasgow B	–	Presumed destroyed
YT	London	–	Destroyed
YU	London	–	Destroyed
YV	London	–	Destroyed
YW	London	–	Destroyed
YV	London	–	Destroyed
YW	London	–	Destroyed
YX	London	–	Destroyed
YY	London	–	Destroyed
YZ	Londonderry	*	
Z	Dublin County	1927–54	Dublin
ZA	Dublin B	1927–54	Dublin
ZB	Cork	–	No information

ZC	Dublin B	1927–54	Dublin
ZD	Dublin B	1927–54	Dublin
ZE	Dublin B	1927–54	Dublin
ZF	Cork B	–	No information
ZH	Dublin B	1927–54	Dublin
ZI	Dublin B	1927–54	Dublin
ZJ	Dublin B	1927–54	Dublin
ZK	Cork	–	No information
ZL	Dublin	1927–54	Dublin
ZM	Galway	–	No information
ZN	Meath		Navan
ZO	Dublin	1927–54	Dublin
ZP	Donegal	1921– *	Letterkenny
ZR	Wexford	1921–	Wexford
ZT	Cork	–	No information
ZU	Dublin	1927–54	Dublin
ZW	Kildare	–	No information
ZX	Kerry		Tralee
ZY	Louth		Dundalk
ZZ	Irish International Circulation Mark	–	No information

Notes to List

AD   Registers for 1903–26; thereafter registration cards only.

AE   Registration cards only, recently deposited privately. Post–1940 cards are expected shortly from the same source.

AI   Early registers for Meath have not survived but the Motor Taxation Dept of the county council has about 80% of vehicle files, including that for AI 1, and many of the remaining 20%, relating to vehicles transferred to other local authorities, are gradually finding their way back to Meath.

AK   Registers for 1903–20; thereafter registration cards only.

AL   Nottinghamshire Archives Office has registers for AL covering the years 1903–20, of which the entries up to 31 Dec. 1903 were published in 'Nottinghamshire Register of Motor Cars and Motor Cycles, 1903', *Thoroton Society of Nottinghamshire Record Series*, XXI (1962), 65–79. From 1921 the office has loose registration forms for all the Notts. index marks (AL, NN, RR and VO) but some of these 'may be out of order ... are difficult to use and appear to have many inexplicable gaps where the records are missing. Certainly where we have been approached by owners in the past for information we have frequently failed to find the relevant records' (information kindly supplied by Notts. Archives Office).

AT   Registers for 1904–18 are at the Transport Museum, High St; Hull City Record Office, 79 Lowgate, have registration cards from 1924 onwards.

AW   Registration cards only.

AZ   The Vehicles (Excise) Act (Northern Ireland) 1972 removed vehicle registration from local authority control to the Government of Northern Ireland, the date of transfer being 1 October 1973. In principle, all local authority registration records should have passed to the Vehicle Licensing Central Office, County Hall, Castlerock Road, Coleraine BT51 3HS, to whom all enquiries concerning Northern Ireland registration marks should be directed. In practice, some local authority registers are in the Public Record Office of Northern Ireland in Belfast or at the Ulster Folk & Transport Museum, Holywood, as noted in the list above.

BA   Later Salford registers are held by the Greater Manchester Police.

BD   The only registers at the Northamptonshire Record Office are those for 1903–21 for the index mark BD. For 1924–78 the office has (unlisted) registration cards for all three Northants index marks (BD, NV and RP).

BE   The Lincolnshire Archives Office has not yet listed records received from the four local registration authorities which existed in the county up to 1974 and relies on a brief note supplied by the registration offices with the documents. According to this, there are complete sets of registration cards for all the Lincoln, Lindsey, Kesteven and Holland index marks but far fewer registers. There appear to be none at all for VL and FW; those for FE are 'Scanty, early... plus a few post-war only'; for BE there are registers to BE 7196 and for FU from FU 4767 to N suffix; those for CT and TL 'Start mid CT's end 1974' (i.e. from 1923); and DO and JL 'DO 1904 to 9990 missing (i.e. 1920–32) otherwise complete to N suffix'. The information given in the list for all the Lincolnshire marks is therefore provisional only.

BF   Under the Motor Car Act, 1903, the Local Government Board allocated BF to Dorsetshire. These letters did not find favour with some motorists and representations were made by the Dorset Automobile Association. The county council applied for a change, which was permitted, and by an LGB Order of 27 Dec. 1904 the mark FX was asigned. The order did not require existing marks to be changed but provided that the owner could have the mark FX substituted for BF on giving notice to the council. The last BF registration allotted was BF 162 on 20 Dec. 1904. 42 of the car owners and 41 motorcycle owners did not change their registration letters but any remaining on the roads on 1 Jan. 1921 were re-registered with FX numbers, since BF was not allocated under the Roads Act, 1920. (Information kindly supplied by the Dorset Record Office.)

BI   Registers for 1933–55 and 1961 onwards; also registration application forms 'from an early date'.

BP   The only registers at the West Sussex Record Office at Chichester are those for BP for the period 1903–20. For 1921–72, however, the office has a quantity of uncatalogued number issue records (which contain less information than the registers) covering all three West Sussex index marks (BP, PO and PX).

BU   Registration cards only.

BZ   See note under AZ above.

C   No registers or registration cards; an incomplete series of vehicle files only.

CA   Registers to 1920; thereafter rgistration cards only.

CC   Registers for 1904–21 and 1952–77; registration cards for 1921–74 (approximately 50% complete); and registration files for 1921–74 (less than 50% survival).

CH   Registers for 1903–21; thereafter memorandum books of new numbers only.

CJ   Registers for 1904–20; thereafter registration cards only.

CO   Registration cards only.

CP   Registration cards only for 1921–77 at Wakefield; registration files for 1921–31 at Halifax.

CR   Southampton City Records Office has a register for CR covering the period 1903–13 and other volumes (not a complete series) to 1919. For TR and OW the office has only the subsidiary application forms for registration (RF(1)), as it has for later CR numbers. None of the series is complete.

CT   See note under BE above.

CX   A register for 1927; otherwise registration cards only.

CZ   See note under AZ above.

DA   Wolverhampton Central Library in fact has a series of seven volumes covering the period 1925–50 for index marks DA, JW and UK, plus an eighth volume for 1955–6. Other volumes were 'returned to West Midlands Police', where they were apparently subsequently destroyed.

DD   Registers for 1921–26; otherwise registration cards only.

DF   Registers for 1926–30; otherwise registration cards only.

DG   Registers for 1929–34; otherwise registration cards only.

DH   Licensing was transferred from Walsall to Dudley in 1957 (index mark FD).

DO   See note under BE above.

DR   Registration cards only.

DU   Registration cards only.

DZ   See note under AZ above.

EC   The Kendal office of the Cumbria Archive Service has only one Westmorland vehicle register as such, containing registration numbers EC 1 to EC 466 and covering the years 1904–09, but has in addition a series of 37 notebooks, deposited by the last manager of the Kendal Motor Taxation Office, registering names and addresses of those issued with EC and JM index marks for road fund licence between 1925 and 1974.

EK   Registration cards only; also registration files for EK 978 to EK 9998 and for JP 1 to JP 9999 (1930s onwards).

EN   Registration cards only.

EP   Registration cards for 1903–74; registers from 1949 only.

EZ   See note under AZ above.

FE   See note under BE above.

FH	In addition to a register of motorcycles for 1910–13 and another for motor-cars for 1912–19, the Gloucestershire Record Office (at its Alvin St branch) has a random sample of registration files for 1957–75 from the City of Gloucester taxation office.
FU	See note under BE above.
FW	See note under BE above.
FX	See note under BF above.
FZ	See note under AZ above.
GR	These records refer only to the transfer of vehicles from other authorities to Sunderland CB (Form RF 16/1).
GV	Registration cards only.
GZ	See note under AZ above.
HD	Registers for 1913–54; otherwise registration cards only.
HP	Registration cards only.
HT	See note under AE above.
HU	See note under AE above.
HW	See note under AE above.
HY	See note under AE above.
HZ	See note under AZ above.
IA	See note under AZ above.
IH	The first two Donegal registers (1903–11) have been transferred to the Archive Centre at the County Library,

Letterkenny, Co. Donegal; others at present still at the Motor Taxation Dept will follow in due course.

IJ   See note under AZ above.

IL   See note under AZ above.

IO   Later registers still in the custody of the Motor Taxation Dept of Kildare County Council.

IP   Registration records are in the custody of the Motor Taxation Dept of Kilkenny County Council; access can be arranged via the County Library, 6 Johns Quay, Kilkenny. The records are incomplete prior to 1950 but thereafter well preserved.

IR   Two volumes, covering the years 1904–23 and 1945–6, are at the County Library in Tullamore; the Motor Taxation Dept of Offaly County Council has later books for 1951–60 and from 1964 onwards.

IU   Later registers are at the Motor Taxation Section of Limerick County Council, O'Connell St, Limerick.

IW   See note under AZ above.

JL   See note under BE above.

JM   See note under EC above.

JP   Registration cards only; also files from 1930s onwards.

JW   See note under DA above.

JX   A register for 1944–47, otherwise registration cards only, at Wakefield; registration files for 1935–57 at Halifax.

JY   Registration cards only.

JZ   See note under AZ above.

KH   See note under AT above.

KI   Registers currently (July 1990) in the custody of the Motor Taxation Dept of Waterford County Council; possible deposit in the County Library (Lismore, Co. Waterford) under discussion.

KM   Registration cards only.

KV   Registration cards only.

KW   Registration cards only.

KY   Registers for 1931–70; otherwise registration cards only.

KZ   See note under AZ above.

LI   Westmeath County Library, Dublin Rd, Mullingar, Co. Westmeath, Ireland, has a volume of driving licences covering the years 1904–12. There may be other material amongst the county council records at County Buildings, Mullingar, but these have yet to be sorted and listed (information kindly supplied by the County Librarian).

LT   The Greater London Record Office has only a single register from the LCC/GLC motor taxation department, covering index marks LT 4001 to LT 4400, issued during the dates shown in the list. The only item to survive for Middlesex (also at the GLRO) is a register covering the years 1916–19 and the areas of Edgware, Kingsbury, Little Stanmore, Great Stanmore, Finchley, Hendon, Wembley and Willesden. This appears to be a register of car owners, rather than a register of index numbers, and the index marks are highly varied. The rest of the London and Middlesex taxation records have apparently been completely destroyed.

LZ   See note under AZ above.

MI   Registration forms only before 1960, fuller information from that date.

MN   Registers from 1966 to the present are at the Vehicle Licensing Section of the Isle of Man Treasury (Government Buildings, Buck's Rd, Douglas); earlier records (1906–65) are at the Manx Museum, Douglas.

MZ   See note under AZ above.

N   Registration mark allocation books only. All other Manchester registration records appear to have been destroyed.

NA   See note under N above.

NB   See note under N above.

NC   See note under N above.

ND   See note under N above.

NE   See note under N above.

NF   See note under N above.

NN   See note under AL above.

NT   Registration cards only.

NV   Registration cards only.

NW   Registration cards only.

NZ   See note under AZ above.

O   The only surviving Birmingham registration records are an incomplete series of files for numbers between O 4000 and O 9999, running from the 1920s to the 1950s.

OI   See note under AZ above.

OW   See note under CR above.

OZ   See note under AZ above.

PO   See note under BP above.

PS   All the registers and registration cards for Shetland have either been destroyed or have passed into private hands. Shetland Archives have an incomplete series of files for 1921–72, together with a photocopy of the first two registers (1904–20), the originals of which are in private hands.

PX   See note under BP above.

PZ   See note under AZ above.

RC   Memorandum books of new numbers only.

RH   See note under AT above.

RJ   See note under BA above.

RP   Registration cards only.

RR   See note under AL above.

RW   Registration cards only.

RZ   See note under AZ above.

SE   Index cards only for SE 3 to SE 5819, i.e. until about 1938, with information added to about 1970.

SM   The Dumfries Archives Centre requires prior written application to use these records, together with the completion of a form attested by two referees.

SO   No registers or index cards; files for each vehicle from SO 1 to SO 7647 (i.e. 1946), with subsidiary information on cards referring to withdrawn files up to SO 9999 (about 1950).

SW   See note under SM above.

SY   This mark was originally allocated to Midlothian County Council and no registers appear to survive from this authority. ASY, however, was used by Linlithgow and there are entries for this mark in the registers from that county now at Edinburgh City Archives (see under SX, the main Linlithgow mark).

SZ   See note under AZ above.

TI   See note under IU above.

TL   See note under BE above.

TR   See note under CR above.

TZ   See note under AZ above.

U   Registers for 1921–42; otherwise registration cards only.

UA   Registration cards only.

UB   Registers for 1931–46; otherwise registration cards only.

UG   Registers for 1932–46; otherwise registration cards only.

UI   See note under AZ above.

UJ   Registration cards only.

UK   See note under DA above.

UM   Registration cards only.

UN   Registration cards only.

UX   Registration cards only.

UZ   See note under AZ above.

VC   Registration cards only.

VH   Registers for 1927–29; otherwise registration cards only.

VJ   Registration cards only.

VL   See note under BE above.

VM   See note under N above.

VO   See note under AL above.

VR   See note under N above.

VU   See note under N above.

VV   Registration cards only.

VZ   See note under AZ above.

WA   Later registers have been retained for the present but not yet
      selected for permanent preservation.

WB   See note under WA above.

WE   See note under WA above.

WI   See note under KI above.

WJ   See note under WA above.

WK   Registration cards only.

WS   This mark was transferred to Edinburgh in 1920, when Leith was incorporated into the city. The surviving registers are from Leith Burgh Council; those compiled after 1920, like the other Edinburgh registers, have apparently been destroyed.

WZ   See note under AZ above.

X   Registration cards only.

XI   See note under AZ above.

XJ   See note under N above.

XZ   See note under AZ above.

YZ   See note under AZ above.

ZP   See note under IH above.

Locations

The following list gives the address and telephone number of each of the locations identified by town only in the foregoing list. The dialling codes are those for use within the United Kingdom and Republic of Ireland respectively and should be prefaced by the appropriate international code when used from other countries.

Aberystwyth   Cardiganshire Record Office, County Offices, Marine Terrace, Aberystwyth SY23 2DE. (0970) 617581.

Aylesbury   County Record Office, County Hall, Aylesbury, Bucks HP20 1UA. (0296) 382587.

Barrow-in-Furness   Cumbria Record Offcie, 140 Duke St, Barrow-in-Furness, Cumbria LA14 1XW. (0229) 831269.

Bedford   County Record Office, County Hall, Cauldwell St, Bedford MK42 9AP. (0234) 63222.

Belfast   Public Record Office of Northern Ireland, 66 Balmoral Avenue, Belfast BT9 6NY. (0232) 661621.

Beverley   Humberside Archive Service, County Hall, Beverley, Hull HU17 9BA. (0482) 867131.

Birkenhead   Central Library, Borough Rd, Birkenhead, Wirral L41 2XB. 051-652 6106.

Birmingham   Central Library, Chamberlain Square, Birmingham B3 3HQ. 021-235 4217.

Bolton	Central Library, Civic Centre, Le Mans Crescent, Bolton BL1 1SE. (0204) 22311.
Bristol	Bristol Record Office, The Council House, College Green, Bristol BS1 5TR. (0272) 222377.
Burton-upon-Trent	Burton-upon-Trent Library, Riverside, High St, Burton-upon-Trent, Staffs DE13 9HD. (0283) 43271.
Bury St Edmunds	Suffolk Record Office, Bury St Edmunds Branch, Raingate St, Bury St Edmunds IP33 1RX. (0284) 763141.
Caernarfon	Caernarfon Area Record Office, County Offices, Shire Hall St, Caernarfon LL55 1SH. (0286) 4121.
Cambridge	County Record Office, Shire Hall, Cambridge CB3 0AP. (223) 317281.
Canterbury	Cathedral Archives, The Precincts, Canterbury, Kent CT1 2EG. (0227) 63510.
Cardiff	Glamorgan Record Office, County Hall, Cathays Park, Cardiff CF1 3NE. (0222) 820284.
Carlisle	Cumbria Record Office, The Castle, Carlisle, Cumbria CA3 8UR. (0228) 23456.
Carmarthen	Carmarthenshire Record Office, County Hall, Carmarthen, Dyfed SA31 1JP. (0267) 233333.
Carrick-on-Shanon	Motor Registration Dept, Leitrim County Council, Park Lane House, Priest's Lane, Carrick on Shannon, Co. Leitrim, Ireland.

Castlebar	Motor Taxation Office, Mayo County Council, Castlebar, Co. Mayo, Ireland.
Chelmsford	Essex Record Office, PO Box 11, County Hall, Chelmsford CM1 1LX. (0245) 492211.
Chester A	Cheshire Record Office, Duke St, Chester CH1 1RL. (0244) 602559.
Chester B	City Record Office, Town Hall, Chester CH1 2HJ. (0244) 324324.
Chichester	West Sussex Record Office, County Hall, Chichester, West Sussex PO 19 1RN. (0243) 533911.
Coventry	City Record Office, Mandela House, Bayley Lane, Coventry CV1 5RG. (0203) 832418.
Cwmbran	Gwent County Record Office, County Hall, Cwmbran, Gwent NP44 2XH. (0633) 838838.
Darlington	Public Library, Crown St, Darlington, Co. Durham DL1 1ND. (0325) 462034.
Dolgellau	Area Record Office, Cae Penarlag, Dolgellau, Gwynedd LL40 2YB. (0341) 422341.
Doncaster	Archives Dept, King Edward Rd, Balby, Doncaster, S. Yorks DN4 0NA. (0302) 859811.
Dorchester	County Record Office, County Hall, Dorchester DT1 1XJ. (0305) 204411.
Douglas	The Manx Museum, Douglas, Isle of Man. (0624) 75522.

Dublin	Archives Division, City Hall, Dublin 2, Ireland. (6797) 111.
Dudley	Dudley Library, St James's Rd, Dudley, West Midlands DY1 1HR. (0384) 456000.
Dumfries	Dumfries Archives Centre, 33 Burns St, Dumfries DG1 2PS. (0387) 69254.
Dundalk	Motor Taxation Dept, Louth County Council, Dundalk, Co. Louth, Ireland.
Dundee	Archive and Record Centre, 21 City Square, Dundee DD1 3BY. (0382) 23141.
Durham	County Record Office, County Hall, Durham DH1 5UL. 091-386 4411
Edinburgh	City Archives, City Chambers, High St, Edinburgh EH1 1YJ. 031-225 2424.
Ennis	Motor Taxation Office, Clare County Council, New Road, Ennis, Ireland. (065) 21616.
Exeter	Devon Record Office, Castle St, Exeter EX4 3PU. (0392) 273509.
Forres	Moray District Record Office, The Tollbooth, High St, Forres IV36 0AB. (0309) 73617.
Galway	Motor Taxation Dept, Galway County Council, Galway, Ireland.
Glasgow	Strathclyde Regional Archives, Mitchell Library, North St, Glasgow G3 7DN. 041-227 2733.
Gloucester	County Record Office, Clarence Row, Alvin St, Gloucester GL1 3DW. (0452) 425295.

Grimsby	South Humberside Area Archive Office, Town Hall Square, Grimsby DN31 1HX. (0472) 353481.
Halifax	Calderdale District Archives, Central Library, Northgate House, Northgate, Halifax HX1 1UN. (0422) 57257.
Hanley	County Reference Library, Bethesda St, Hanley, Stoke-on-Trent ST1 3RS. (0782) 215108.
Haverfordwest	Pembrokeshire Record Office, The Castle, Haverfordwest, Pembrokeshire, Dyfed SA61 2EF. (0437) 763707.
Hawarden	Clwyd Record Office, The Old Rectory, Hawarden, Deeside, Clwyd CH5 3NR. (0244) 532364.
Hereford	Record Office, The Old Barracks, Harold St, Hereford HR1 2QX. (0432) 265441.
Hertford	Hertfordshire Record Office, County Hall, Hertford SG13 8DE. (0992) 555103.
Holywood	Ulster Folk & Transport Museum, Cultra, Holywood BT18 0EU. (0232) 428428.
Hull	City Record Office, 79 Lowgate, Hull HU1 2AA. (0482) 222015.
Huntingdon	County Record Office, Grammar School Walk, Huntingdon PE18 6LF. (0480) 425842.
Inverness	Regional Archivist, Kinmylies Building, Leachkin Rd, Inverness IV3 6NN. (0463) 234121.

Ipswich	Suffolk Record Office, Gatacre Rd, Ipswich, Suffolk IP1 2LQ. (0473) 230000.
Kendal	Cumbria Record Office, County Offices, Kendal, Cumbrian LA9 4RQ. (0539) 721000.
Kilkenny	Kilkenny County Library, 6 Johns Quay, Kilkenny, Ireland. (056) 22021.
Kirkwall	The Orkney Library, Laing St, Kirkwall, Orkney KW15 1NW. (0856) 3166.
Leicester	Leicestershire Record Office, 57 New Walk, Leicester LE1 7JB. (0533) 544566.
Leigh	Wigan Record Office, Town Hall, Leigh WN7 2DY. (0942) 672421.
Letterkenny	County Library, Letterkenny, Co. Donegal, Ireland. (074) 21968.
Lerwick	Shetland Archives, King Harald St, Lerwick, Shetland ZE1 0EQ. (0595) 3535.
Lewes	East Sussex Record Office, The Maltings, Castle Precincts, Lewes, East Sussex BN7 1YT. (0273) 481000.
Limerick	Limerick Regional Archives, The Granary, Michael St, Limerick, Ireland. (061) 40777.
Lincoln	Lincolnshire Archives Office, The Castle, Lincoln LN1 3AB. (0522) 525158.
Llandrindod Wells	Powys Archives, Library Headquarters, Cefnllys Rd, Llandrindod Wells, Powys LD1 5LD. (0597) 826060.

Llangefni	Anglesey Area Record Office, Shirehall, Llangefni, Anglesey, Gwynedd LL77 7TW. (0248) 750262.
Lochgilphead	Dept of Admininistration, Argyll & Bute District Council, Kilmory, Lochgilphead, Argyll PA31 8RT. (0546) 2127.
London	Greater London Record Office, 40 Northampton Rd, London EC1R 0HB. 071-633 6851.
Maidstone	West Kent Archives Office, County Hall, Maidstone, Kent ME14 1XQ. (0622) 694363.
Manchester A	Greater Manchester Record Office, 56 Marshall St, New Cross, Manchester M4 5FU. 061-832 5284.
Manchester B	Archives Dept, Central Library, St Peter's Square, Manchester M2 5PD. 061-234 1980.
Matlock	Derbyshire Record Office, County Education Dept, County Offices, Matlock, Derbys DE4 3AG. (0629) 580000.
Middlesbrough	Archives Section, Exchange House, 6 Marton Rd, Middlesbrough, Cleveland TS1 1DB. (0642) 248321.
Monaghan	Motor Taxation Office, Monaghan County Council, County Offices, The Glen, Monaghan, Ireland. (047) 82211.
Navan	Motor Taxation Dept, Meath County Council, County Hall, Navan, Co. Meath, Ireland.
Newbridge	County Library, Newbridge, Co. Kildare, Ireland. (045) 31486/31109.

Newcastle-upon-Tyne	Northumberland Record Office, Melton Park, North Gosforth, Newcastle-upon-Tyne NE3 5QX. 091-236 2680.
Northallerton	County Record Office, County Hall, Northallerton, N. Yorks DL7 8AD. (0609) 780780.
Northampton	Northamptonshire Record Office, Delapre Abbey, London Rd, Northampton NN4 9AW. (0604) 762129.
Norwich	Norfolk Record Office, Central Library, Norwich NR2 1NJ. (0603) 761349.
Nottingham	Nottinghamshire Archives Office, County House, High Pavement, Nottingham NG1 1HR. (0602) 504524.
Oldham	Central Library, Union St, Oldham OL1 1DN. 061-678 4654.
Oxford	Oxfordshire Archives, County Hall, New Rd, Oxford OX1 1ND. (0865) 815203.
Plymouth	West Devon Area Record Office, Unit 3, Clare Place, Coxside, Plymouth PL4 0JW. (0752) 264685.
Portlaoise	Motor Taxation Dept, Laois County Council, County Hall, Portlaoise, Co. Laois, Ireland.
Preston	Lancashire Record Office, Bow Lane, Preston PR1 2RE. (0772) 54868.
Reading	Berkshire Record Office, Shire Hall, Shinfield, Reading, Berks RG2 9XD. (0734) 875444.

Roscommon	Motor Taxation Office, Roscommon County Council, Roscommon, Ireland. (903) 26100.
Ruthin	Clwyd Record Office, 46 Clwyd St, Ruthin, Clwyd LL15 1HP. (08242) 3077.
St Helens	Local History and Archives Library, Gamble Institute, Victoria Square, St Helens WA10 1DY. (0744) 24061.
Salford	Archives Centre, 658-662 Liverpool Rd, Irlam, Salford M30 5AD. 061-775 5463.
Sheffield	Sheffield Archives, 52 Shoreham St, Sheffield, S1 4SP. (0742) 734756.
Shrewsbury	County Record Office, The Shirehall, Abbey Foregate, Shrewsbury, Shropshire SY2 6ND. (0743) 252851.
Sligo	Sligo County Library, The Courthousee, Teeling St, Sligo, Ireland. (071) 42212.
Smethwick	Local Studies Centre, Smethwick Library, Warley B66 1AB. 012-558 2561.
Southampton	City Records Office, Civic Centre, Southampton SO9 4XR. (0703) 832251.
Southend	Essex Record Office, Southend Branch, Central Library, Victoria Avenue, Southend-on-Sea SS2 6EX. (0702) 612621.
Stafford	Staffordshire Record Office, Eastgate St, Stafford ST16 2LZ. (0785) 223121.
Stirling	Central Region Archives Dept, Unit 6, Burghmuir Industrial Estate, Stirling FK7 7PY. (0786) 50745.

Stranraer	District Museum, 55 George St, Stranraer DG9 7JP. (0776) 5088.
Swansea	West Glamorgan Area Record Office, County Hall, Oystermouth Rd, Swansea SA1 3SN. (0792) 471589.
Taunton	Somerset Record Office, Obridge Rd, Taunton TA2 7PU. (0823) 278805.
Tralee	Motor Taxation Dept, Kerry County Council, Moyderwell, Tralee, Co. Kerry, Ireland. (066) 22300.
Trowbridge	County Record Office, County Hall, Trowbridge, Wiltshire BA14 8JG. (0225) 753641.
Truro	Cornwall Record Office, County Hall, Truro TR1 3AY. (0872) 73698.
Tullamore	County Library, O'Connor Square, Tullamore, Co. Offaly, Ireland. (0506) 21113/21419.
Wakefield	West Yorkshire Archive Service, Registry of Deeds, Newstead Rd, Wakefield WF1 2DE. (0924) 295982/290900.
Walsall	Walsall Local History Centre, Essex St, Walsall WS2 7AS. (0922) 721305.
Warwick	County Record Office, Priory Park, Cape Rd, Warwick CV34 4JS. (0926) 412735.
Waterford	Motor Taxation Dept, Waterford County Council, Waterford, Ireland.
Wexford	Motor Taxation Dept, County Hall, Wexford, Ireland.

Wicklow	Motor Taxation Dept, Wicklow County Council, Wicklow, Ireland.
Winchester	Hampshire Record Office, 20 Southgate St, Winchester SO23 9EF. (0962) 846154.
Wolverhampton	Central Library, Snow Hill, Wolverhampton WV1 3AX. (0902) 312025.
Worcester	Record Office, County Hall, Spetchley Rd, Worcester WR5 2NP. (0905) 766352.
York	Archives Dept, Art Gallery Building, Exhibition Square, York YO1 2EW. (0904) 651533.

Philip Riden

Born in 1952, Philip Riden was educated at Chesterfield School and St Edmund Hall, Oxford, where he was an open scholar and took a first in Modern History in 1973. After three years as a research student at Nuffield College, he taught briefly at Exeter University before moving to his present post at the University of Wales College of Cardiff, where he has been Lecturer in Local History in the Department of Extra-Mural Studies since 1977. Mr Riden is the author of two standard textbooks on sources for local history, as well as numerous more specialised books, articles and pamphlets. Besides archives and their use, his other major areas of research include urban history and the history of the iron industry.

Philip Riden's interest in motor vehicle registration records developed after his acquisition of a 1966 Daimler $2^1/_2$ V8, which he is currently restoring.